THE GIFT OF HELPING

THE GIFT OF HELPING

Myra Chave-Jones

Foreword by John Stott

God has appointed in the church...helpers...
(1 Corinthians 12:28 RSV)

Inter-Varsity Press

Inter-Varsity Press
38 De Montfort Street, Leicester LE1 7GP, England.

Quotations from the Bible are from the New International Version,
©1978 by the New York International Bible Society, published in Great
Britain by Hodder and Stoughton Ltd., unless otherwise stated.

First published 1982

Reprinted 1983

British Library Cataloguing in Publication Data
Chave-Jones, Myra
    The gift of helping.
    1. Pastoral counseling   2. Peer counseling in the church
    I. Title
    253.5   BV4012.2

    ISBN 0-85110-444-4

Phototypeset in 10/11pt Palatino
by Nuprint Services Limited, Harpenden, Herts.
Printed and bound in Great Britain by Collins, Glasgow

*Inter-Varsity Press is the publishing division of the Universities and Colleges
Christian Fellowship (formerly the Inter-Varsity Fellowship), a student
movement linking Christian Unions in universities and colleges throughout the
British Isles, and a member movement of the International Fellowship of
Evangelical Students. For information about local and national activities in
Great Britain write to UCCF, 38 De Montfort Street, Leicester LE1 7GP.*

CONTENTS

FOREWORD

'Help!' The word springs naturally to our lips if we find ourselves in a desperate situation. If we've had an accident, or are being carried out to sea by a strong current, or are trapped in a burning building, we put our lungs to the best possible use and shout for help.

Yet if our problem is spiritual or moral rather than physical, many of us cannot bring ourselves to admit that we need each other. We need the Lord Jesus, of course. We are quite prepared to sing old hymns like 'I could not do without thee, O Saviour of the lost' and 'I need thee, oh, I need thee, every hour I need thee'. But need each other? Surely not. Paul wrote, 'my God will meet all your needs according to his glorious riches in Christ Jesus' (Philippians 4:19). Would it not, then, be derogatory to Christ to confess our need of human help? Is not his grace sufficient?

I myself used to think and argue that way. Many Christians do. Only last week, as I write, a lady came to see me, whose marriage was falling apart. She and her husband, though living under the same roof, had not communicated with each other for years. It was obvious that they both needed help to understand each other. 'Had they sought help before?' I asked. 'No,' she replied. 'I'm a Christian. I'd be ashamed to. I've been taught that Christ can help me.'

This kind of reluctance to seek help is sometimes accompanied by a reluctance to help others. After all, if *we* are supposed to cope on our own, shouldn't *they* also?

But over the years I have come to see that these attitudes have more in common with Stoicism than with Christianity. *Autarkeia* was one of the Stoics' favourite virtues, 'self-sufficiency' or 'independence'. We Christians, however, should be honest and humble enough (for humility is only another word for honesty) to admit that we need each other.

Paul did. Strong Christian leader that he was, he depended much on the loving support of his friends. During his final imprisonment he wrote expectantly of the second coming of Jesus; but meanwhile he longed for the coming of Timothy: '...Do your best to come to me quickly...Do your best to get here before winter' (2 Timothy 4:8–9, 21). And previously, when he had been in great distress, 'conflicts on the outside, fears within', he wrote: 'But God, who comforts the downcast, comforted us...' Many Christians think the quotation ends there. Indeed, the text seems to support their view that in all our needs the divine comfort is enough. But what Paul actually wrote is 'God...comforted us *by the coming of Titus*' (2 Corinthians 7:5–7). Thus Paul needed the helping hand of friends, and so do we.

That is why I welcome this book by my old friend from Cambridge days, Myra Chave-Jones. To begin with, it is thoroughly biblical. It is also wise. She is a practising psychotherapist, who has worked during the past seven years in association with Care and Counsel, a Christian service in London, of which she is now Director. Moreover, her book is in keeping with the 'philosophy' of Care and Counsel, which is to avoid relieving Christians and churches of their responsibility to care, and instead to help them to care better themselves. Myra avoids both the professionalism which wants to leave everything to the experts and the amateurism which would dispense with them altogether. Between these extremes, she recognizes that there are many situations of need in which ordinary Christians can learn how to love and serve people with sensitivity.

Here, then, is a valuable primer on how to be a 'Help' or a 'helper'. It is very human, and therefore often humorous. It is also very practical, abounding in real, or imaginary, examples. I warmly recommend it.

JOHN R. W. STOTT

SETTING THE SCENE

They have been closeted in that room for three hours; the midnight oil has long since burnt low; empty coffee mugs are littered around, the voices are quiet now and there are long pauses that have a despairing quality about them. All the pros and cons of the problem have been gone over this way and that, several times; and there seems nothing left to do but go, rather unsatisfactorily, to bed.

But the problem is no nearer resolution. The obvious answers do not seem to be of any use and there is a sense of deadlock. Even in bed, new problems seem to emerge, such as:

'Where is God when it hurts?';

'A Christian ought not to feel like this';

'I prayed about it and was so sure it was God's will';

'I wonder if anyone understands how awful this feels.'

As the participants in the discussion go their separate ways until next time, there is often a sense of pressure and anxiety. The would-be helper is very burdened by his friend's pain, and feels there *must* be some answer. Tomorrow he will get someone else in who might be more experienced. Indeed, he would phone now if it were not so very late.

Let me say at once that sitting up into the night trying to sort something out is usually a bad thing to do. Everything looks much blacker and more hopeless around midnight. Decisions may be made which look quite different in the cold light of day. It is also sensible to remember that we are unlikely to say anything new or see new aspects of the problem when we have discussed it for more than two hours. A wiser thing would be to pray about it and then get some sleep (or let the other person get some sleep), because it will still be there in the morning, awful though it may seem. Another fact of life is that when the current problem has been solved, there will be many more before we eventually reach the Celestial City.

As we wend our way through life we all meet people who are in need, whether we are looking for them or not. We ourselves are in need from time to time. This book is addressed mainly to people, especially in the student world, who want to respond helpfully to the cries of others; people who want to be encouragers and comforters to those who are worried or in distress.

1

THE HELPER

Do you remember the story of Christian's journey from the City of Destruction to the Celestial City, told so vividly in Bunyan's *Pilgrim's Progress*? One of the first obstacles which Christian encountered was the Slough of Despond. He 'being heedless did suddenly fall into the bog'. He struggled and wallowed, 'grievously bedaubed with dirt', until he saw a man called Help who asked him what he was doing there and why he had not looked for the steps. 'Give me thy hand,' said Help, and he drew Christian out of the miry slough, set his feet on sound ground and bade him go on his way.

No more is said about Help. He was not seen again and we know nothing of him personally. This was a brief encounter, but without it Christian may never have continued his journey. Help was someone who knew the terrain, had a watchful eye for travellers and the knack of being in the right place at the right time. He was also conspicuously unobtrusive. He is a splendid example for the rest of us who would like to be Helps.

Nowadays 'counselling' is very much in fashion. Personally, I do not like the word. It implies some specialist knowledge or some superior position. Of course, there is a place for people with professional skills who are Helps in situations of emotional complexity. For the purposes of our present discussion, however, I would like us to consider the case of ordinary people who simply want to befriend, comfort and encourage other people with whom they are naturally in contact.

People have been talking and sharing their problems ever since human beings have been around. It is a normal activity which anyone can do. It is specifically undergirded

11

with scriptural authority. 'Bear one another's burdens, and so fulfil the law of Christ' (Galatians 6:2 RSV).

Having said that anyone can do it, however, obviously some people do it better than others. Some seem to have an instinctive ability to respond more easily than others, and not everyone has the same gifts. Nevertheless, we can all learn to help in ways which are more sensitive and effective. In this, as in most other things, practice makes perfect.

Knowing ourselves

We cannot launch into carrying other people and their burdens until we have some knowledge of our own strengths and weaknesses. If we try to do so, there is every likelihood that Help will fall into the bog along with his friend.

Some people regard 'contemplating one's navel' with a certain amount of scepticism and say it is an unhelpful occupation. They say we should have our eyes fixed on Jesus and on the needs of others, and not be concerned with selfish introspection. This is true, but not the whole truth. If I am driving a car, I am not totally preoccupied with the destination map and the other traffic. A safe journey also requires awareness of the state of my own vehicle. What is the condition of the tyres, the petrol, oil, water, battery, and the engine as a whole? But it is difficult to examine ourselves objectively, and we need external aids and mirrors.

The help of God's Word

Our first aid is God's Word: 'The word of God is living and active. Sharper than any double-edged sword, it penetrates even to dividing soul and spirit, joints and marrow; it judges the thoughts and attitudes of the heart' (Hebrews 4:12). As we turn it over constantly in our minds, we test our emotional reactions to obedience, to other individuals, to money and possessions, to personal integrity, to sexual behaviour. There is no secret double standard or hypocrisy which can be hidden away. 'Everything is uncovered and laid bare before the eyes of him to whom we must give account' (verse 13).

This can sound alarming and uncomfortable, but it helps us to be honest. We need to read on as we keep it in mind. 'For we do not have a high priest who is unable to sympathize with our weaknesses, but we have one who has been tempted in every way, just as we are – yet was without sin' (verse 15). He knows all about us and understands our inner struggles and Achilles' heels, and with loving strength he yearns to be a Help to us. He knows the circumstances of our life, and why we are as we are, and he has a tremendous investment in helping us to overcome that which is wrong and to encourage that which is weak. 'Let us then approach the throne of grace with confidence, so that we may receive mercy and find grace to help us in our time of need' (verse 16).

Self-assessment

Our second aid to self-knowledge is a deliberate assessment of ourselves. It is necessary to spend time thinking about this with some care (which is why we may seem to spend a disproportionate amount of space on it here). If Help does not know himself, it is very possible that he may become unhelpfully enmeshed with the problems of his friend.

Each of us has his own self-image.

'I am a good sportsman.'

'I am very shy.'

'I am not particularly academic.'

'I hate my huge feet.'

'I don't like people who flirt.'

'I wish I could take responsibility.'

As we make our list and ask deeper questions about the items, we find that some of them reveal more than we thought at first sight. 'Why am I so shy?' 'Why do I fear what people are thinking?' 'In whose company am I particularly ill at ease?'

As we unpack this problem we may gain deeper insight which we can bring out into the open for prayer and help. For instance, we may gradually become aware that somehow we seem to attract an undue number of people with big problems which absorb a great deal of our time and energy. This may lead us to ask a few questions about the significance of the situation. Could it be that somehow our own morale is boosted when people need us? Do we need to be needed as a way of reassuring ourselves that we are loved? Do we somehow feel so responsible for them that almost consciously we keep them in a state of dependence on our care? Is all this helping that we do actually a statement of our own need as much as it is about other people's?

Our own need could be for some sort of reassurance derived from their dependence, or for some sense of identity which we acquire from being a helper. Or it might be that by comforting someone else we are trying to comfort some deep unhealed wound of our own; that some inner ache is relieved when we soothe someone else's pain.

Another similar situation is the inability of some people to say 'no' or set limits. We feel we must be at everyone's beck and call, constantly and endlessly giving, even at great personal inconvenience. The irritation that this eventually engenders is smothered (except that it may show itself in headaches, stomach pains, skin conditions, *etc.*). We use scriptural texts to explain our behaviour, quite forgetting that sometimes the Lord himself withdrew from the clamouring crowds who needed help, because he had to attend to his own inner needs (Luke 6:12). But somehow we seem to be involved in an endless activity syndrome.

Are we justifying our existence?

Are we afraid that people will not love or trust us any more if we do not meet their demands?

The truth is that if we are to be Helps we must be genuinely free to say either yes or no. Help has his own needs. It is unrealistic to imagine that anyone can be a limitless absorber of other people's problems. It is important

14

to examine these things, because otherwise there is the real possibility of the blind leading the blind and both ending up in the ditch.

Another less dramatic possibility is that a *folie à deux* may develop. Help and the other person grow to need each other and cannot survive independently; then neither can move on to new areas of growth.

Our self-image is important because it determines our behaviour and affects the way people react to us. Other people may not agree with our assessment, but it is *our* view of ourselves, and not theirs, which is the motivating factor. No amount of bland contradiction or simple reassurance is likely to alter the view we have built up over the years.

Many Christians believe that the proper attitude for a Christian is a *poor* self-image, and that a sign of a spiritually mature person is his constant self-denigration. This is a misunderstanding.

The proper attitude for a Christian is described graphically in Ezekiel 16:1-14. Ezekiel was told by God to go to the people of Jerusalem and tell them this oriental allegory. Their origins were mongrel and undistinguished; they were like an unwanted baby girl, unloved and 'thrown out into the open field', a prey to whatever was roaming around. Then the Lord passed by and saw this wretched sight, and said to the unpromising infant, 'Live!' He enabled the child to grow and develop into 'the most beautiful of jewels'.

Later on he passed by again and made a covenant of adult love with this beautiful woman. 'I gave you my solemn oath and entered into a covenant with you,' declared the Sovereign Lord, 'and you became mine.'

In confirmation of his intent, the Lord dressed her in fine and costly clothes, adorned her with ornaments and jewels, and fed her delicately. She 'became very beautiful and rose to be a queen' whose fame spread far and wide because 'the splendour I had given you made your beauty perfect'.

Who was this queen? No-one special. Where did she come from? Nowhere in particular. How did she acquire all this acclaim? It was a free gift from someone who loved her; a statement of his goodness. It would be a total betrayal if she denied it all, went around in sackcloth and ashes, threw away her jewels and refused her food. Everything she was, was a reflection of the generosity of her Lover, and a pointer to his greatness. Her gratitude, enjoyment, and recognition of it would be one way of expressing her thanks. She would never forget her origins, but that would only go to enhance her appreciation.

This balance of attitude is the proper stance for a Christian. We have been created in the image of God and redeemed and forgiven by Jesus Christ, and are being changed in personality by the Holy Spirit to become new creatures. God now sees us as his sons and daughters (Galatians 4:4-7) whom he knows and cares for personally. This should give us a *good* self-image!

We do not deny our God-given human abilities, opportunities or successes. We accept and acknowledge them with a thankful spirit. We can also admit to the parts which need to be changed. We are secure in the knowledge that God's resources of love and patience are available, within which growth and change are possible. If we sweep the unacceptable things under the carpet or refuse to acknowledge them, there is no chance that they can be dealt with. We shall also be less able to be Helps to others.

Help from friends
Our third aid to self-knowledge will be other people in whom we can place our confidence: people who have demonstrated their ability to be impartial, wise and discreet. In the growing friendship between us we may have revealed inner thoughts and feelings which we hide from most other people. Our friend will have reacted to them with encouragement, rebuke, or questioning, and we will have been able to assimilate his responses. He will have told us about the effect that we have on other people (which we cannot know adequately by ourselves) and whether or

not we are being true to ourselves. We shall weigh up his observations against our own thinking to get a rounded view.

In his book *Why Am I Afraid to Tell You Who I Am?* John Powell says, 'I can only know that much of myself which I have had the courage to confide in you.' The rest is vague, unproved feeling or fantasy.

Take, for instance, the way we look at people. At times when we are feeling embarrassed, frightened or angry, we find it difficult to look someone straight in the face. That person will either pretend he has not noticed, or he will comment on what we seem to be doing. If he does the latter, we shall be required to acknowledge our feelings, deal with them or face them in some way, and thus 'know' them. It is painful to have them out in the open. It is easier to take avoiding action by averting our glance.

It is also difficult for us to respond directly to the disturbed feelings of the person to whom we may be talking. So we often pretend we have not noticed because we are not sure if we can handle the situation. Or else we just ignore it all.

There are times when encounters like this can be faced carefully and sensitively so that both people can understand and 'know' themselves better. A little comment such as 'You sound annoyed/disappointed/hopeful' can lead on to further exploration. Other people can pick up tones in our voice or a look on our face of which we ourselves are often unaware.

We all have secret doubts and thoughts which are fairly important to us, but which seem too childish or dangerous to share with another person. Because they seem important, they *need* to be shared. It is the very sense of importance which can be out of proportion. To expose some of these thoughts may be risky, but it is valuable to be able to get them out into the open, look at them, and thus 'know' them for what they really are.

Professional help

Finally, some of us may need professional help ourselves. This may be the hardest of all. It may seem to imply weakness and failure. Actually, to ask for help is a sign of greater health than to battle on with constant failures, trying to control and understand a situation which is simply too big for us. When the advice of older friends, and all our best endeavours, including spiritual resources, seem to fail, we may need to look more deeply at the whole thing in a professional way.

It is the opinion of some people that if we are right spiritually there will be no problems, or at least nothing that cannot be put right fairly quickly by prayer and Bible study. This is not necessarily the case, and can be quite a cruel thing to say. Some problems have occurred because of faulty learning patterns and unfortunate life-experiences for which we ourselves are not responsible. Such difficulties can be built deeply into our psychic and emotional constitution and are beyond our conscious control– some types of depression for instance. We are not responsible for their causation, but we *are* accountable for what we do with these difficulties and for whether or not we make them an excuse for continuous inadequacy.

FURTHER READING
Why Am I Afraid to Tell You Who I Am? by John Powell (Fontana).

2

APPROACHING THE PROBLEM

If we want to offer constructive help and real support, it is important to approach our friend's problem from God's perspective. We shall look in this chapter at some factors Help needs to bear in mind.

God's timing

Many Christians bring their problem to the Lord in genuine willingness and earnest wish for his will. But the answer does not seem to work overnight. Relationships go wrong, the illness is not cured, the loneliness persists, or there is no indication about what to do in a problematical situation. Is prayer worth while? Does God really care? Is he really omnipotent? These questions can carry with them real pain.

Sometimes this pain is simply due to our own limited vision and a 'Jim'll Fix It' attitude. On this popular television programme, people, mostly children, ask Jimmy Savile to procure some special delight for them, such as a visit to a place normally inaccessible, or an interview with some important person. Jim seems to have amazing influence and can achieve things which would be impossible to other mortals, with no expense spared. The appeal of the programme seems to lie in Jim's 'fairy godfather' image. Sometimes we treat God as though he were a fairy godfather.

Our sense of time sometimes confuses our perception of answered or unanswered prayer. A small baby is aware only of the present moment. 'Tomorrow' is a concept far beyond his understanding. If his mother does not come *at once* to respond to his cry, he becomes panic-stricken and desperate. He thinks she has gone beyond recall and has abandoned him. This makes him feel insecure, unwanted and worthless. Because of the limitations of infancy he is unable to understand time, her faithfulness and her acute awareness of his need.

We all have to learn about *trust*, when there seems to be no immediate and recognizable answer. So often we behave like spiritual or emotional babies. The life-experience of a faithful parent (or of God) and the *practice of trust* enable us to grow into calm and mature people. But the lesson is sometimes very hard to learn. Moreover, we may have learnt it once and then have to start all over again on a different level. This is the way character – human and Christian character – is built (James 1:3-4).

God never holds us in limbo just for the fun of it. It is always to teach us lessons about trust and a wider perception of time. Just as a human baby learns new experiences each day, in relationship with its loving and responsible parents, so a Christian will be learning all the while about life, in relationship with his heavenly Father. He will be growing more and more to understand and trust the goodness and generosity and faithfulness of God. Within that over-all care he will also be able to accept discipline and restraint, without which parental generosity becomes harmful indulgence.

In many passages in the Bible the phrase 'the fullness of time' is used. That simply means that the moment for action has come in the human time-scale, although the whole operation has been endlessly complete in God's eternal and timeless reckoning. T.S. Eliot describes this in *Burnt Norton:* 'Time present and time past are both perhaps present in time future, and time future contained in time past.' Much of our pain would be unnecessary if we could only learn to stay at 'the still centre', the place where our spirit is in touch with eternity and can therefore remain unruffled by the whirl of daily events, though not untouched by them It is like being in 'the eye of the storm'.

Guidance

There is the difficult question of guidance. Sometimes our requests for guidance are merely a disguised attempt to avoid the responsibility of making choices and decisions. God will not do things for us which we are well able to do for ourselves. We must learn to pray and ask for things which stretch and develop the human personality and discernment which he has given to us.

At the same time we must be aware of our need to live totally within God's known general will, revealed in the Bible. Although God knows the details of our life, he does not expect us to live in bondage as though every small decision were of vital importance. He has given us free will, the faculty to discern and to be responsible. He expects us to use them prayerfully within the over-all knowledge of God. It is our responsibility to get to know him through his Word so that we shall have freedom to move about without fear, within his will. An adult son does not have to consult his father about minutiae. He is free to express himself, and he knows what is acceptable and what is doubtful or wrong.

Some of our prayers are so heavily coloured by our own fantasies that they seem to us to be genuine when in fact they are simply a projection of our own will. We need to ask ourselves some penetrating questions about the content and motivation of our prayers. *Why* do I ask for this? What would it mean to me personally if I did not get it? Can I live without it in freedom and emotional fitness? Am I trying to manipulate or bribe God? Is this a prayer of uncomplicated trust in a wise and good Father, which leaves the results in his hands?

Some of us have been guilty, at times, of convincing ourselves that we know what the will of God is, when actually we have created a situation by our *own* will.

People have often felt confused about this subject of God's guidance. It is not easy to be sure: often we can be sure only in retrospect. We can only be as honest with ourselves and with God as we know how, listening to sensible and balanced friends, willing for God's ultimate will to be done, prepared to step out and experience new areas of faith. Help has to learn these lessons himself, just as he is helping his friend to learn them.

Guidance is a continuous process which is far more like exploring a relationship than searching for some secret coded message. Our heavenly Father has told us repeatedly in his Word that he is longing for our greatest good and deepest joy, that he wants us to know him and his blessing in our individual personal life. There can be no possible doubt that his plans for us are to prosper us and not to harm us (Jeremiah 29:11).

Growing pains

Sometimes, however, our interpretation of such promises leads us to expect life to be one long beautiful morning with everything coming our way. Not at all! Too much sunshine makes a desert. But nonetheless we somehow get the idea that if pain and discomfort are around and if we are puzzled over God's guidance, something must be wrong. At times the very process of growth *involves* pain and discomfort.

This contemporary world has some unrealistic ideas about pain. Although we watch physical and emotional pain *ad nauseam* on the television, we do everything we can to avoid experiencing it ourselves. We have come to regard it as something which should not be allowed, something unmitigatedly negative. True, pain was not in the original plan of creation, but like everything else it has its positive side. Pain, both physical and emotional, holds within it the potential for healing, the motivation for change and the opportunity for growth. We must learn to distinguish between the pain caused by a broken relationship of love with the Lord, and the discomfort caused as we are growing more into the life of the Spirit and less into the life which is dominated by the values of our own nature and the dictates of the world around. We are not disembodied spirits, and so the ordinary events of life are often the context of our deepening relationship with God. We need to be reminding ourselves about all this, as we try to be Helps to other people. We are all growing and reaching out towards maturity. The fact that we are in pain about something does not *necessarily* mean that we have stepped outside our relationship with God. Discomfort is not always to be equated with wrong. The Lord Jesus himself was in discomfort many times as he grew in maturity and as he wrestled with temptation and other people's sin.

Whose pain?

If we are suffering with a friend we must be careful to distinguish between bearing the pain *for* him and bearing it *with* him. If we seem to be taking it over *for* him we may be depriving him of the opportunity to get to grips with the causative problem and to call it by its real name.

For instance, my friend may be complaining of some injustice (real or imagined) done to him. Because he is my friend I may feel outraged and want to set about redressing the wrong or consoling him. That may indeed be desirable to some extent; but before I start doing it I have to think about the issues. People are often the architects of their own distress. Why did this situation come about? Was there some subtle setting-up of this situation before it exploded? Is this event typical of a pattern in the person's life?

Rowena was in floods of tears and Patsy was trying to help. The trouble was that Nigel was obviously going out with another girl now, though he had not actually said so. Rowena had been interpreting his comments and gestures to mean that their friendship was something very special and leading towards engagement, although he had not been specific. The whole situation was made worse because this was the third time she had been let down in this way. Patsy was fond of Rowena and was, herself, so upset to see her distress that she felt quite inclined to seek Nigel out and have a straight talk with him. Someone ought to tell Nigel that his behaviour was totally unscrupulous and dishonest!

As she turned it over in her mind, however, she began to realize that she herself would be much relieved by the straight talk with Nigel. She also began to realize that Rowena was fairly desperate to have a permanent boyfriend and that she had been fantasizing about the relationship a fair amount. Rowena seemed to be somewhat insecure emotionally, so she had been clinging to Nigel too urgently and creating a pressure which made him feel trapped. The failure of Rowena's two previous friendships had only increased her sense of insecurity and her need to cling. A vicious circle was rapidly becoming established.

The best way for Patsy to be a Help to Rowena would be to stand by her in love and thoughtful practical care, encouraging her to endure and learn from this painful situation rather than ignore or resent it, to acknowledge and admit her own contribution to the breakdown in relationship rather than blame Nigel or men in general, and to accept and incorporate this unpleasant experience into life's total pattern rather than split it off into a secret compartment to which she could retire from time to time for a private orgy of self-pity. Thus Rowena would be helped to grow as a whole person, spiritually, emotionally, and perhaps even in physical health.

My attempts to lessen my friend's pain, because I feel it so acutely, may be just what he is looking for; but perhaps the time has come when he needs to be taking steps to lessen his *own* pain. So I must ask, What is my role in all this? Am I taking over the situation in the manner of a suffocating mother whose desire is to protect her offspring from all hurtful contact with this wicked world? Or am I being an 'enabler', standing by supportively while he works it out for himself, and thereby grows and develops into a more mature person?

Part of the emotional pain may be the sheer frustration of not being able to resolve the problem and thus get rid of it. It goes against the grain to have to submit to something we do not enjoy. We feel defeated, bewildered and angry in addition to feeling other emotions which the problem itself may arouse.

It is sometimes specially hard for Christians to accept that there is no solution to some problems. There *must* be a way out: there *must* be an answer. How can a situation be left unresolved? So the would-be Help finds himself under strong pressure to say something effective or to find a solution just because uncertainty is so difficult to bear. To some problems, such as death or some of the suffering of innocent people, there is no solution in this world. The only helpful thing is to listen, to care and to be there. Inability to give the 'right' answer does not necessarily signify failure.

The real need

Sometimes Help needs to penetrate beneath the surface problem and identify the underlying problem that may have caused it.

Garth was being very unsociable because of an appalling relationship with his stepmother. He had come drifting down to breakfast one day, late and bleary-eyed as was his custom at home, and she had gone for him out of all proportion to the offence. She was constantly complaining about him and to him, and it seemed that he could not do anything right. He thought the acrimony was due to the step-relationship, and had decided he just had to put up with it. His friend Keith, who was staying with him, pointed out a contrast between his behaviour at college and his behaviour at home. At college he always managed to arrive for his first lecture on time, and even to snatch breakfast first. But at home he fell back into habits of childhood, expecting to be called and reminded, and automatically hung around until he *was* reminded. After all, that's what home was for – so he thought. He had always done it. He was scarcely aware that by this he was goading his step-mother whom he knew to be punctilious and precise. It was so much easier for Keith to see this, as an onlooker, than for

Garth who was a main participant in the interplay. Keith had resisted the temptation to enter the fray on behalf of Garth, but had analysed the situation and drawn Garth's attention to his own part in it.

Help must always be on the watch for the underlying problem which may be compounding the superficial circumstances. It is generally a mistake to listen to someone's complaint and take it at face value. The person who is complaining will obviously see things from his own viewpoint and the story will be coloured accordingly. Help, if he is to be a true helper, must therefore have some degree of detachment and impartiality. His friend may experience this as lack of understanding, so this situation must be handled with some sensitivity.

Help must also avoid the pitfall of wanting to press his own interpretation of the situation. He may be wanting to speak from some personal experience of his own, but that may not be appropriate to his friend's case. Thus Help has to tread a careful path between over-identification with this friend and over-enthusiasm about his own experience.

Spiritual or emotional?

Some Helps attribute every problem to a spiritual cause, and feel that more intense prayer or Bible reading or laying-on of hands will solve the difficulty. This may be over-simplistic. Of course, in the last analysis all our problems, whatever they are, originate in our fallen nature. Many of our sorrows are caused by our own deliberate fault, and in that case we must identify the problems and accept personal responsibility. But some of our sorrows arise because we are more sinned against than sinning. In this case we have to identify the problem, be prepared to forgive where necessary, and be responsible for our own movement towards change and maturity. We cannot blame other people for our misery. When we are no longer children, we are responsible for our own development and for what we do about these difficulties.

26

Some of Help's friends may interpret healing as instantaneous gratification of desire, possibly in a spectacular manner. God does sometimes strengthen our faith by dealing with us in this way. He also strengthens our faith by teaching us about endurance and patience. We have to be prepared for either. Help has to distinguish between genuine faith and the impetuous desire (found in the secular world) to take the waiting out of wanting. Help must be concerned about the whole person, rather than focusing solely on an 'emotional' problem or a 'spiritual' cause. It is seldom possible to put problems into any exclusive category. Social conflict, physical illness, emotional difficulty and spiritual needs are all connected, and when something goes wrong in one area the others are affected automatically. Each human being is a unified whole.

If someone says that he is unable to pray or that he has no sense of God's presence, that *in itself* does not indicate a spiritual problem. It would be foolish to assume that some sin or devotional neglect is the cause without having heard a fuller description of the situation.

Standards and values

It might be timely to make some general observations here about the fact of temptation. This word sounds more appropriate to Puritans or Victorians than to twentieth-century people. Temptation is presented to us nowadays as something frivolous and unimportant, naughty but nice – like a new brand of delicious but fattening chocolates or a perfume whose allure is irresistible.

Help may be asked for his opinion when someone is toying with temptation. So he needs to think about some of the issues.

First, none of us is as free to choose as we like to think. Environmental, psychological, and spiritual influences have damaged our freedom, but we are still free to some extent, and responsible for the choices we make. They cannot all be explained away by some so-called 'psychological theory'. We are all responsible people and are accountable to ourselves, to other people and to God for the way we conduct ourselves.

Secondly, we must distinguish between temptation and sin. There are some thoughts and fantasies over which we have no control: they come unbidden and spontaneously. They are not in themselves sin. Only when we entertain and play with them do we allow them to establish themselves as a reality. Temptation then passes into the realm of sin. But there is a difference between the two. Martin Luther is reported to have distinguished between them by saying, 'You can't stop the birds flying over your head, but you can stop them making nests in your hair.'

Thirdly, we are all under heavy, subtle indoctrination all the time to adopt the standards and values of the world. Sometimes we just do things because everyone does it and it feels right. Help must remember that there are many people around nowadays who do not know God and therefore are unaware of his standards and values. Even some Christians come into this category and need instruction.

Fourthly, Help must remember that when we want something very much indeed we are very skilful at persuading ourselves that wrong is right. We can convince ourselves even against our own judgment that a course of action is permissible. Somehow, the Primal Scene, the first recorded conversation of sentient man, is enacted all over again (Genesis 3:1-6). A voice within says, 'Has God said "No"? He didn't really mean that. It would spoil my life totally if I were to be denied that thing. Think how fulfilled and experienced it will enable me to be. I shall be so much more use in the world if I do have it.'

With this argument we cease to recognize temptation for what it is. The devil becomes an angel of light, and the battle is lost. Help must refuse to collude with the voice within. The resultant course of action may make him unpopular or incomprehensible to his friends. He must, of course, be loving, courteous and sensitive throughout, and very prayerful, remembering that 'we are not contending against flesh and blood, but against... spiritual hosts of wickedness' (Ephesians 6:12 RSV).

In his famous *Screwtape Letters* C.S. Lewis portrays the senior devil Screwtape writing from his extensive experience of human nature to his nephew Wormwood, a junior devil learning the tricks of the trade. Screwtape says, 'Like all young tempters you are anxious to report spectacular wickedness. But do remember, the only thing that matters is the extent to which you can separate man from the Enemy [God]. It does not matter how small the sins are, provided that their cumulative effect is to edge the man away from the Light and out into Nothing. Murder is no better than cards, if cards can do the trick. Indeed, the safest road to Hell is the gradual one – the gentle slope, soft underfoot, without sudden turnings, without signposts.'

The cost of healing
One essential condition of healing is that the person with the problem must actually *want* to change. Help must remember this when he talks with his friend.

We have the example of Lot's wife (Genesis 19:15-26). Men sent from the Lord came to warn Lot of the impending destruction of Sodom and strongly urged him to leave everything in a hurry. Lot hesitated; he had a good life and many friends in Sodom. There were some rough types but he personally had done well there and expected a fairly settled future. He was persuaded only by the urgent pressure of these strange visitors who wanted him to make a clean break with the place and get right away. Even so, he didn't want to go *too* far away. He would leave, but he would go to a small town just outside the danger zone. He made it out of the city, just in time, with his even more reluctant wife and daughters.

But his wife's heart was in Sodom. She did not want to leave and go to some unknown and doubtless uncomfortable

29

place. She did not want to change and be helped. The devil she knew was better than the devil she did not know. So she followed behind, dragging her feet and feeling more and more reluctant. Then she stopped, her body expressing her thoughts. She turned round and stood looking back, gazing longingly at her real home – and she became enveloped again in the life of Sodom, only this time it was 'burning sulphur'.

There are people for whom the cost of change is too appalling. They cannot reach forward in faith and hope. Their heart is set in the known patterns of the past, and in spite of verbal assertions that they want release, they in fact become like pillars of salt. They want to be relieved of the *results* but not the *cause* of the problem. It is only the Holy Spirit who can be their Help, but even he will not force an unwilling rescue.

There are others who do not want to change because their problem serves a useful purpose. It is a sure way of attracting attention and making people care. They think that if they have nothing with which to engage people's concern no-one will notice them, and that is painful to contemplate. Help needs to recognize the underlying dynamics of this situation and convey the necessary attention without allowing himself to be manipulated.

A vital question, therefore, in the helping process is 'Do you want to be made well?' Help must know the quality of his friend's answer to this question or he may be banging his own head against a brick wall.

There was a man who had been lying beside the pool of Bethesda for thirty-eight years (John 5:1-15). That had become a way of life for him. He had made a few attempts initially to struggle free from the crippling condition, but now he was just living with it. Perhaps he had a lean diet sometimes and was cold on occasions; but he was a familiar figure there, and people would not let him starve. He had no major decisions to make and there was always someone to talk to. His paralysis had become his identity.

30

Then one day the Lord Jesus was standing there. Those clear searching eyes seemed to penetrate right into his inner life which was overgrown from years of slackness and inattention. 'Do you want to get well?'

What a question! How could he reply to such a challenge in one honest moment? So he blustered with a fumbling explanation, but he knew his questioner would see through it. All those years of lying there had given him plenty of opportunity to observe people. He recognized that this unknown man was different. Jesus had come straight to the point with an unusual aura of authenticity. Somehow the invalid knew that this man could see a part of his life that was vital, personal and relevant. Suddenly that part began to matter, whereas before it had been in semi-consciousness. In one great burst of hope, faith and incredible courage he knew he wanted to be freed from the half-life that he was living. He heard the command, 'Get up! Pick up your mat and walk!'

He could have responded, 'I'm not the only one: there are plenty of people around in a worse state than I. Just look at them!' But he said in effect, 'Yes, I am what you can see'. At once he was cured; he picked up his mat and walked, and his Help slipped away in the crowd.

Not only did his body perform actions it had not done for many years, but his emotions were confronted with new situations. Now he had to think about earning a living, making decisions, and taking responsibility for himself instead of being dependent on other people. He also had to face moral issues of right and wrong which he had not really bothered about too much before. His second brief encounter with the Stranger pinpointed verbally the earlier implications about wholeness and the relationship between the life of the spirit, the emotions and the body: 'See, you are well again. Stop sinning or something worse may happen to you.' I wonder whether he ever looked back over his shoulder at 'the good old days', when the risks of decision-making always rested on someone else's shoulders?

The cost of healing is considerable. Change is not easy. It requires courage, total co-operation and commitment on the part of any person who is asking for help.

FURTHER READING
Where Is God When It Hurts? by Philip Yancey (Pickering and Inglis).

3

THE TASK OF LISTENING

Sometimes we hear someone say, 'Thank you so much for all you have done,'and we feel slightly surprised. We have not *done* anything. We have only listened. Yet somehow, through the *way* we have listened, the person has found help.

The listening atmosphere
Words are only one method of communication. There are the facial and bodily expressions, the tone of voice, the hesitations and changes of subject, the moments of spontaneous emotion, the style of presenting a problem or asking for help, the omissions and the silences. We must try to hear *all* that is being transmitted and to understand its significance.

This is active listening. This is the sort of 'giving attention' which facilitates relief. It is listening which has been described as 'a kind of prayer'. One ear is available to the speaker, *hearing* in a very deep way what he is meaning. The other ear is listening to what God may have to speak into this situation. This sort of listening takes time, concentration and self-discipline and therefore some sacrifice. It may be boring, difficult or even painful.

Receptive listening conveys certain attitudes to the other person. It makes him know that he is valued and what he wants to say is important because he is saying it. Many of the deepest things that people feel and think are never said because there is no-one who will receive them with the attentive care that they require. It may be only in the calm security of the listener's ear that a person can let off the steam of pent-up emotions. It may be that he needs a 'father confessor' with whom he can share some anxiety and guilt.

33

or that he wants a sounding-board against whom he can test out some of his reactions. He may not be asking for advice or intervention of any sort. When he has been provided with an atmosphere in which he can spread out his problem in whatever way he feels appropriate, and has been helped to look at it, he will reassemble the pieces and go away feeling helped (although the listener has not 'done' anything).

Obviously, in order to listen to people in this way one has to be *available*. It is not simply a matter of being available physically. It is about being free from preconceived ideas and prejudices. This does not mean that we do not have our own views – sometimes held quite strongly – but it does mean sufficient detachment from them to be available to pick up the full meaning that the other person is trying to convey.

Communication is a two-way process. There is not much point in talking if no response is forthcoming. The person looking for help wants to know that you have received his message and that you have understood its content and meaning. You are walking along with your friend when he says, 'I am afraid I might fall into this hole.' If you reply, 'Don't be ridiculous! Of course you aren't going to fall into this hole', you have responded to only part of the message. You have reacted to the facts of the situation and ignored the emotions. Your friend may react by feeling rebuffed or hurt. His fear that he may fall into this hole may relate to his experience with a previous hole, or it may be warning him about his shoes, or some disequilibrium in his semi-circular canals, or his general state of apprehension about everything.

The importance of feelings

Feelings are a very important part of our total person. They are something equivalent to the 'temperature' of the personality. On a physical level the thermometer will be a guide to whether we have a fever which needs attention. On an emotional level our feelings will indicate whether some part of our psyche needs special attention. It is important to pay attention to what an indicator is registering. Physical or emotional pain is a similar indicator which will guide us to a suitable helper.

There are some Christian people who advocate that we should ignore our feelings. They probably mean that we should not be dominated by and subservient to them. But we ignore them only at our peril. They are usually an accurate guide to our own internal economy and will tell us whether and where adjustment is necessary.

Lorna was asking for help because her feelings had all gone dead and she was not interested in anything. There seemed to be no obvious reason. As she thought over her recent life in detail, with Ruth, she began to live again the events which culminated in an abortion six months before. She had been appalled to find herself pregnant and saw only one way of dealing with the problem so that she could continue with her studies. She gritted her teeth and got on with it. She had not expected the aftermath that this massive suppression of feelings would produce. She had not told anybody at the time: it is not the sort of thing you discuss. Anyway, what was done could not be undone, so there was no point in crying about it.

Ruth saw that Lorna was now carrying around inside her a solid mass of powerful feelings which had no outlet. But gradually Ruth managed to create an atmosphere in which Lorna felt safe. Her secret would not be leaked and she would be accepted for herself in spite of everything. Ruth persisted gently in encouraging her to talk about the heavy burden which was crushing her feelings. Lorna began slowly to expose the previously barricaded past. As she re-experienced her feelings, which had been so firmly pushed away, all the pain, fear and shock began to come to the surface: feelings about Bob which she did not quite under-stand now – a mixture of anger, indifference and scorn; and her own reaction to herself – deep regret, bewilderment and a strange sense of loss. It took many weeks of tears, talk and misery until Lorna could reach the place of forgiveness and peace.

Feelings are a vital part of our human constitution. In no circumstances can they be disregarded, denied or suppressed without exacting a heavy toll and coming up in some other unexpected form. Often our body pays the price, and we start glandular fever, skin trouble, respiratory difficulties, headaches, digestive disorders, eating problems and other physical manifestations.

Practical hints

The ability to listen well is a skill worth cultivation. The world is too full of people who are anxious to talk, but there are many people who are yearning for someone to listen to them. Help will spare time to attend without distraction. That in itself makes a person in trouble feel supported and valued.

Sometimes Help experiences a great desire to *do* something. I cannot urge strongly enough that adequate listening *is* doing something. There are times when some additional activity is needed, but the immediate inclination to rush into action should be resisted strenuously. The reason is, first, that when the whole story has been told, the person asking for help may see the problem in a different light. Secondly, until Help has had time to understand the full impact of the story he cannot know what is the best thing to do.

So listen. Be quiet: don't interrupt. No-one can be listening and speaking at the same time. When we are speaking we are not listening. Many of us have to exercise a real practical discipline in keeping our mouths closed for any long period of time! *It does not matter if there is a silence for a minute or two*. It gives both people an opportunity to reflect on what is being said. A conversation is not the same as a tennis match. In conversation, the 'ball' can be allowed to rest from time to time. Wait until you have been given a signal to speak. People will usually look up, or ask 'What do you think?', or make it obvious that they are now ready for some reaction. But a mere pause is not always Help's signal. He needs to be very careful not to intrude on a reflective silence.

If we ask questions or urge the speaker on, it often indicates that we have become caught up with our own ears (the story as I am hearing it) rather than the speaker's eyes (the story as he sees it). Questions are useful only if they attempt to elucidate something *for Help,* or to draw the speaker's attention to some discrepancy. They should be simple questions, preferably open-ended. But when the speaker is in full flood, questions are out of place even if Help does not follow the argument. They can deflect the speaker from his point.

Be attentive and interested in what the other person is saying (but not inquisitive). Look at him and train yourself to remember the details. He will know if you are watching the door or the clock or if your mind is somewhere else. Concentration requires effort.

He may have burst in at an impossibly inconvenient moment. It is much more caring to say that you can't listen now but you will be free later on in the day, than to be distracted and give only half an ear to a problem which he feels is serious. If you have only a limited time to spare, tell him so and give him the choice about whether to speak now or come back. It is important to make some boundaries, but they need not be inflexible if the problem turns out to be really urgent.

Listen to what is said between the lines. Make a mental note of what you see as well as what you hear.

'John's voice was quiet and he spoke calmly, but his eyes looked black and his knuckles were white as he gripped the chair.'

'Mary told me all about the incident in detail, but she did not mention herself once.'

'David wanted to come at four o'clock, but he forgot and turned up at quarter to five.'

37

What do these things tell you?

Try to remain dispassionate. If you allow your own emotions to get out of hand in this situation, you may be unable to be a Help. You may feel grieved or angry on behalf of the other person, but it is *very important* to distinguish between your emotions and his. It is, of course, appropriate to weep with those who weep. The point is to keep your *own* emotions in a secondary place.

I remember that on one occasion tears of sympathy welled into my eyes as I was listening to a young man tell his story. He stopped suddenly with 'Oh, am I upsetting you? I'm so sorry.'

I sensed that he was being much more guarded in what he said after that, because I had allowed my emotions to intrude before he was ready.

Don't be judgmental. If someone is sharing something which he knows or you know to be wrong, do not show disapproval or shock. He is sharing it with *you* because he trusts you not to reject him. He needs your understanding. He needs Help to bring him to the place of confession, reconciliation, restitution or forgiveness. The fact that Help does not *show* disapproval does not mean that he is condoning wrong-doing. It means that he is accepting the person who is speaking, and remembering that we have all sinned.

It is appropriate to be shocked by some of the things which one hears. Help is not being asked to accept everything blandly. He *is* being asked to control his reactions.

Be sure you understand the sense in which a word is being used. Recently I was speaking with someone about 'that big word psychotherapy', referring to its costliness in terms of time, money, commitment. 'Oh yes, I do know the word', she said, referring to its length. 'I have a degree in psychology!'

Perhaps a more usual misunderstanding could arise about the use of the word 'bad'. If someone says he feels bad, he could mean he feels uncomfortable, guilty, unhappy, ill, worthless, embarrassed, or even something else. Other similar words are 'anger', 'guilty' and 'love'. These words are in such common use that often it does not occur to Help to find out exactly what they are intended to mean.

Stay with the speaker's subject and do not respond to his story by giving a parallel one of your own. You may have something interesting to say, but he does not necessarily want to hear it. *His* situation is the one at issue. Help may have had a very similar experience, but he can best use it now by conveying his sympathy and applying his imagination, rather than by relaying details of the actual event.

Do not give advice. Most people do not want it and will not use it. It is unhelpful to say, 'If I were you I would . . .' or 'I think you ought to . . .', because you are not me, and your view of what I ought to do is *yours*. What you need to understand is *my* view. The only real value of good advice is that it makes the person giving it feel better. (Of course, advice which relates to factual knowledge – for example, which course of study to follow for a particular career – is a different matter.)

Don't argue. It is sometimes difficult not to become argumentative when some strongly held point is at issue. If you find yourself ranging in an opposing camp to your friend, you may only harden his previous attitude. Try to understand what his point of view means to him. ('*Why* is he so upset? *What* does this represent to him?')

Don't seem to preach. At all costs be humble and gentle. Loving, careful attention is more effective in the long run, and that may include a quiet and authoritative statement of God's revealed thoughts from Holy Scripture about a situation.

Don't probe, unless it is essential for greater understanding, and unless your friend is willing. Help must be on the alert for the slightest hint that he has gone too far, or is on dangerous ground. This hint could be a change of position or a stiffening of voice, or, more obviously, a change of subject. Help must check and be sure that the friend wants to go on.

The relationship between a person and his Help

There are certain factors which determine the choice of a Help. There are often unstated but specific expectations. The person in need may select a Help in whom to confide because he knows he is likely to receive sympathy, an identical viewpoint, or reinforcement of his position. Another will choose his Help because of the personal integrity and lifestyle which that person represents. Another person will want a selection of Helps, each of whom may represent a different position.

It is valuable to have some idea of the expectations on both sides, because they do influence the situation. Some simple question such as 'What are you wanting from me?' or 'How can I help?' would make the expectations clearer.

It is essential to respect complete *confidentiality*. Nothing is worse than to break someone's confidence by sharing it at a prayer meeting, or in some other well-intentioned situation.

Another important factor is Help's *genuineness*. He will try to be honest and avoid saying things which do not ring true to his own real position. That may involve acknowledging his own lack of knowledge or his prejudices. It may mean he has to admit that he is too closely involved in the situation to be dispassionate.

Possibly he may have to do some gentle *confrontation* about inconsistencies or even sinful behaviour.

'You say you want to succeed, but you put the standard so high that you are fairly sure to fail.'

'You are smiling, but what you have said does not sound amusing.'

'You are leading the Bible study, but it does not sound as though you are taking that piece seriously.'

'You did that really well. Why do you find it so hard to take the proper credit?'

Confrontation is a delicate task. We must remember that the purpose is to help, not to condemn; to heal, not to stir up trouble. Help will therefore give support as he confronts and enables the person to share the problem more deeply.

Many a tangled web has been woven when Help has tried to help someone of the opposite sex. The helping relationship is inevitably close and emotionally charged, and in that situation it makes sense for Help to stick to his own sex. Of course this is not a hard and fast rule: it depends on how well the people know each other. But if it is important to someone to find a Help of the opposite sex, Help would want to ask some searching questions about the reason.

The person who finds himself cast in the role of Help may feel flattered that someone has come to consult him. But it is important for him to understand the biblical concept of the body of Christ (1 Corinthians 12:12-27). We are each an integral part of the whole. No-one is superior and no-one expendable. Sometimes Help is in a position to give to someone else; on other occasions Help himself will need to receive.

Out of your depth

How does Help know when he is out of his depth? The answer is, 'When he can't touch the bottom.' If he is not a very accomplished swimmer he is wise to stay within his depth if he is alone. If Help finds he is floundering, he usually *is* out of his depth and should stop. On many occasions the situation warrants the inclusion of some wiser head, but the one important requisite in any situation is to be there, lovingly, unobtrusively and faithfully.

The Holy Spirit is our Counsellor (John 14:16), and he helps us be sensitive both to the situation and to ourselves within the situation. He will teach us as we go. If there are other experienced people within reach from whom we can learn (such as college chaplain, pastor, older Christian), we should take every opportunity to do so. Help may also need

41

to refer his friend on to such a person. Sometimes Help feels himself being dragged down, and becoming engulfed in the problem or the person. This is always a danger signal. If Help does not know what is dragging him down, he would be better out of the situation. It is a false – and dangerous – sense of spiritual commitment that makes us unable to withdraw or say no. Obviously no conscientious Help will suddenly pull up the ladder without an explanation.

Strangely, it is sometimes very helpful to the person with the problem to have a faithful feedback about how he comes over. Help's quality of life helps him to know it is done in truth (and not just in exasperation). Help's friend may be able to use this particular interaction as a growth point. If not, an opportune question might be, 'Do you want to be healed?', or 'What do you really want in this situation?' One very practical way of controlling the situation is to set, *and keep to,* a limited amount of time for problem discussion. Very little can be achieved by spending endless hours going over the ground (except in the case of bereavement or where someone is really working through a problem).

Emergencies

Even when Help is presented with a sudden emergency it is still important to be aware of what is happening. Panic spreads rapidly. Is the urgency generated by a dangerous external situation, or by the explosive feelings of the person concerned? It is often useful to listen quietly and thus defuse the panic to some extent. If Help genuinely has no time to spend immediately with this emergency call, he will, of course, do his best to sum up the situation quickly and find another Help, or return to the problem as soon as he can. Whatever else, he must *keep calm.*

FURTHER READING
The Wisdom to Listen by Michael Mitton (Grove Booklets).
Restoring the Image by Roger Hurding (Paternoster).

4

WORKING ON THE PROBLEM (I)

In this chapter and the next we shall focus briefly on some common problems that Help may encounter: depression, lack of sense of identity, work and personal discipline, loneliness, bereavement, failure, drugs and alcohol, the feeling of defeat experienced by some Christians, and relationships with parents. Because many problems concern sexual relationships, we shall look at that area in the chapters 6 and 7.

Depression
Depression arises from a variety of causes. It can be chemical imbalance which needs medical help. It can be due to the person's emotional constitution which has been growing during his life history. It is sometimes due to stress and pressure of circumstances or work. Often it follows on the loss of some significant relationship or major change.

For example, when a student first goes away to university or college, all the well-known landmarks of school life and seniority have suddenly gone. He finds himself in a strange town, among strangers, and feeling 'new' in a huge hall of residence. He has no family life, and a programme which he himself is largely responsible for organizing. Some students find this exciting and challenging, but others may be precipitated into a depression because their sense of security is threatened.

One symptom of depression is inability to make lively relationships; there is a great sense of being unloved and a failure (although that sense may have no basis in reality). Naturally, this extends to the relationship with God, and includes the feeling that God does not care any more and that the media of communication in Bible reading and prayer have closed down. A depressed person often has trouble about eating (too much or too little) and sleeping, and often feels very lethargic. Here we have a typical example of a person's social, emotional, physical and spiritual aspects working together.

How can we be Helps in this situation? It is frequently very worrying to have to stand by and watch a friend struggling with this black monster. We feel so helpless. No words seem to bring comfort or make any impact on the situation. We need to be aware that feelings of depression communicate themselves to other people and that we, as Helps, are exposed to them. The only thing for Help to do, in most situations, is to be there, quietly unruffled, consistently and unobtrusively loving and understanding, and calmly trusting in the Word of God, even though the depressed person cannot appreciate that. Sometimes a little act of practical thoughtfulness conveys more about God than does a text of Scripture.

Sometimes people seem to be under the impression that a Christian should never be depressed. They have an image of joyful singing and triumphant praising all the time. Closely following that image is the implication that any deviation from the path of 'victory' implies failure in living a proper Christian life. That may be so in some cases. None of us can live for very long on spiritual reserves. We must be renewing our unclouded relationship with God all the time.

A censorious attitude, however, is inappropriate for Help. Many great saints through the ages have struggled with periods of painful depression and even suicidal thoughts, among whom are Elijah, Job, David and even Paul, who was under such great pressure that he despaired of life (2 Corinthians 1:8). Anyone who is sensitive is liable to normal depression. It is also part of the costly ministry of prayer and engaging with evil which most of us know too little about.

FURTHER READING
Coping with Depression by Myra Chave-Jones (Lion).

No sense of identity

This problem of identity is very undermining. It makes people feel like a piece of flotsam and jetsam, expendable, uncertain and impersonal. It affects their relationships, decisions and sense of direction. They do not feel that they have any impact on society or on other individuals.

The person who is struggling with this problem may well need to seek professional help if it is severe. Certainly, Help should keep within his own boundaries, simply encouraging, befriending and supporting him. This in itself can produce surprising results. It could well be that the person in need has always encountered criticism and rejection and felt that no-one has ever tried to reach out to him and understand him, so he has lived inside himself, not daring to share his inner thoughts and probably thinking no-one wanted to know. Maybe he is right. Perhaps no-one did want to know until Help came along.

Gerald was in such a position. He was an only child. His father was extremely strict and found children a nuisance, so Gerald clung more to his mother. His parents' marriage was not happy and his mother found in Gerald the responses which should have come within the marriage relationship. She indulged and pampered him and he was always a loner at school because he did not know how to relate to the other boys. He felt awkward and different, but was not close enough to anyone to compare himself with them or discover what other boys were thinking and doing. He compensated for his social ineptitude by his good academic performance.

Eventually Gerald arrived at university not really knowing what he wanted to do or what he was good at. At first he was embarrassed at the friendliness of Jeremy, the man in the next room. But he noted that this man persisted, without being intrusive, when all the other initial encounters had ended in nothing. He felt strange as he had some conversations with Jeremy, almost like a child discovering what was appropriate to do or to feel. If only someone had helped him with all of this years before, he thought. It was not easy either for him or for Jeremy, and they often had misunderstandings.

When Help meets someone who feels inadequate, inferior and insecure, he knows that his task is to be continuously encouraging, supportive and affirming, without implied criticism or heavy expectations. Slowly and patiently, Help will try to assist his friend on to the solid ground of a secure identity from which he can look at life from a new and healthier viewpoint.

Obviously, the Word of God has something relevant to say to this situation, and the oriental allegory of Ezekiel 16 will come into our minds (pp. 15-16). Any really sound sense of identity must come initially from our knowledge of spiritual acceptance with our Creator and Father. Because we are sons and daughters of God, we have a new nature, a new confidence, a new sense of purpose and a new identity. Our confidence does not rest on our own position, our 'fine clothes and jewels', but on the changeless character of the God who gave them to us. This is something we all have to learn more and more. Even Help has to learn increasingly to rely and trust deeply and in practical detail on the One who describes himself as Truth and Life.

It may be a hard and long-term task for a person who is unsure of his identity to begin to develop it. Nevertheless, just because he may be the product of unfortunate experiences for which he is not primarily responsible, he is not absolved from the need to grow. Everyone is responsible for the way in which he uses his talents and personal equipment, whether he has ten or only one (Matthew 25:14-30).

Work and personal discipline
One of the biggest adjustments for a new student is the area of self-discipline over work. Normally the school pro-

gramme has been fairly structured and the timetable clearly marked. Now, however, the student is expected to manage his own workload with the maximum freedom and minimum supervision. All these new freedoms are intoxicating – new societies to join, new topics for discussion and new friends to make. The temptation is to spend too much time enjoying the lack of constraints until suddenly panic sets in when virtually no work has been done towards the end of the first term. A similar panic begins to set in again in the months before finals and students start living on Valium and sitting up till the early hours in a ferment of anxiety.

How is Help to help someone who is in a panic about work, or any other issue? The first thing is to keep calm! Panic is remarkably infectious and spreads like wildfire. Whatever the situation, it isn't the end of the world. Secondly, Help must help his friend to see if there is anything practical to be done to redeem the situation, and if so, to do it with as much courage as possible. Thirdly, Help must share with his friend the always-important question: What can be learnt from this? Panic and anxiety often thrash around saying 'Someone must do something', but the real issue is, 'I must get hold of this situation, and get hold of myself – and having *got* hold, keep hold.'

The friend is really learning about how to manage himself. Until now, someone in the outside world made the rules. Now he has to make his own and take responsibility for the results. This is the challenge of accepting mature adulthood, and sometimes it is quite stretching. It means deciding priorities and standing by them; it means declining some things which are good in favour of things which are better; it means setting realistic and attainable goals and making sure they are reached.

In the course of all this there will be some trial and error, learning by experience, adjustment, flexibility and increased understanding of individual limits. There is no prescribed recipe for learning how to manage ourselves. Each person is different and must discover for himself how

47

much sleep he needs, and the balance between work and recreation. He himself must accept responsibility for the results, whether they are good or bad, and be accountable for them.

These are the positive and constructive steps in self-discipline. That is an unpopular word these days, but very much in fashion, nonetheless! While I was working on this chapter, I stayed in the same hall of residence as a hundred young Welsh footballers. When they arrived, my heart sank. Now for noise, chaos and total confusion, I thought. Not being a follower of these matters, I associated football with broken glass, shouting, ripped train seats and any sort of mindless hooliganism. But I was in for an education. I learnt to distinguish the players from the fans. These fellows had one objective in mind – to win the cup – and to that end they trained, played and studied with little respite for a week, glorying in their tremendous physique. Added to all that, they were espousing a rigorous degree of self-discipline which had wide ramifications in their lifestyle.

Sensible self-discipline is a quality without which no-one can live a purposeful life, but it does require motivation, application and perseverance. It can be difficult to maintain if everyone round us is following the philosophy that says, 'I shall do what I feel like doing, when and where I feel like it.'

Help cannot achieve self-discipline for his friend. He can only set an example by his own unobtrusive, cheerful attitude to himself, and encourage others in their attempts. Obviously, Help cannot be much help unless he has come to grips with some of these basic issues himself. They are to some extent bound up with his own sense of identity and direction.

One important factor in all this is his attitude to the Christian Union and its activities. Help must remember that the best witness for the Lord Jesus Christ is that he should get as good a degree or qualification as is within his grasp. There is no credit in being adorned with 'Jesus stickers' and consistently handing in late work of poor quality because so much time has been spent evangelizing or attending meetings.

Somewhere a balance has to be drawn between conflicting loyalties. This is often difficult because of understandable pressure from members of the CU to support it totally. The atmosphere in the CU can be extremely warm and supportive and may seem like a substitute family. This can be really important for people who have no experience of a good family and home, and can constitute an additional pressure to become totally involved.

Students sometimes tend to live in a Christian ghetto. Most of their friends are members of the CU. Sometimes, without knowing it, much of their Christian faith is in fact based on Christian fellowship and has not been worked out personally. This will not be much good when it has to stand up in the hard world outside. It is therefore extremely important for the student to have a place in the local church as well, where he can be taught by and have fellowship with people who are older in the faith and in life experience.

FURTHER READING
The Fight by John White (IVP), ch. 10: 'Deliverance from drudgery'.

Loneliness

Some students feel terribly lonely. They come up to college or university with the fantasy of utopia. After the first flurry of society-joining, things settle down; but if they do not manage to get on to a satisfactory bandwagon quickly, they begin to feel lost and lonely. They miss not going home at the end of the day, and someone asking how they have been getting on. They stay in their rooms feeling empty and alone and do not know how to make contact with other people. They watch or listen to other people who sound jovial and able to cope with the situation. They begin to feel that everyone else appears to be clever and successful. It is only a

49

short step to tears, loss of appetite and depression.

Loneliness is an awful feeling of inner emptiness which can be accompanied by sadness, discouragement, restlessness, anxiety and an intense desire to be wanted by someone. Almost any relationship would be better than this involuntary isolation. Loneliness may be caused simply by absence of friends, or it may be lack of skill in relating to other people, brought about by a sense of being personally uninteresting and a feeling of not belonging or of being rejected. Either way, our Christian Help has an opportunity to reach out a hand. Obviously the ultimate objective is to introduce the lonely person to the Lord and include him in the Christian family, but it is a bit facile to try to use this as an immediate means of primary evangelism. This student is a person to be valued, not a scalp to be hunted!

Some people are lonely because they do not know how to communicate with others. They may be reluctant to reveal themselves for fear of being criticized and hurt, or for fear of intimacy and being known; so they build invisible barriers around themselves. The pain of loneliness for such people is almost as great as the fear of reaching out to others. They need to be approached with great sensitivity.

Other people are lonely because they are basically hostile, feeling resentful and cheated and with a chip on their shoulder. Their attitude to life is negative and complaining, so not surprisingly people are driven away and the loneliness and hostility are reinforced. This hostility can sometimes be traced to a hidden hatred of themselves. Other people are lonely because of their own self-centredness, intolerance or demanding attitudes which drive people away.

There are many lonely people around. Some try to drown their loneliness in work or sport, drugs or sex, incessant noise and activity or a variety of other ways. The watchful Help (who is not so busy that he does not notice) may be able to detect an isolated person who makes periodic but usually not very successful attempts to reach out to others, or the one who does not seem to be able to establish warm and comfortable relationships. He may try gently to come alongside and eventually enable the person to share the problem. He will manage to do this only by the consistent quality of his thoughtful caring in many small, practical ways. He thereby 'earns the right' to speak more openly to his friend when the time comes.

There is something very hard about confessing to being 'lonely'. It sounds like some nasty social disease, although everyone is lonely at some time or other. Having admitted to loneliness, it may be possible to unpack the situation a bit more and discover one of the causes. Some loneliness (for instance, after bereavement) cannot be changed immediately, but where the basic problem is a negative attitude, this may be discussed and explored and a more positive stance encouraged gradually. The helping spiritual dimension is obvious as lonely people relate to themselves and to other people, or wrestle with the human gaps in their life which cannot be filled.

Perhaps it would be good for all of us to develop the poise of being comfortably alone from time to time. The world is busy, and does not encourage the building of inner resources which are really the ultimate measure of integration.

Bereavement

Death does not usually bother students. It is not a normal part of their scene. But if it comes it leaves everyone shattered. The prospect of death touches the deepest parts of our being, especially when it is our own death or that of someone close. It goes straight to that excruciating area of separation. It also raises the mysterious questions about the meaning of life, and priorities to which we normally give scant attention. What is Help to do when he is trying to comfort someone in a situation which is entirely unknown to him? If it is something of which he has had no experience, he need not be afraid to say so.

51

The emotions in bereavement follow a foreseeable pattern, however, and it would be useful for Help to know about them. The initial phase is shock and incredulity and then refusal to believe or accept this unwelcome news. This then gives way to waves of intense emotional pain which seem to be engulfing. Little things like a phrase of music, the sight of a tree or a photograph – anything that causes associations – will set it off again. This may be accompanied by profound weeping and withdrawal from company or work. There may well be anger against God, doctors or anyone involved as the sad person struggles to come to terms with the inevitable.

'What sort of God is this?'

'Those doctors were just careless.'

'He ought not to have gone rowing that day.'

There may also be some feelings of guilt, 'If only I had been there.' 'If only I had listened.'

Certainly the lethargy and lack of interest in routine things are signs that some absorbing piece of urgent work is taking place within the psyche, so that there are fewer resources available for everyday concerns.

After a time, the bereaved person will want to ruminate endlessly about his lost one. He will go over and over events, conversations, holidays, letters and photographs. This is the time for an upsurge of interest in life after death. It is basically an emotional effort to achieve some personal reunion. Spiritists make capital out of this phase of emotional need. Their ministrations do not help the eventual process of healing: they just keep the wound open, quite apart from the fact that God's Word expressly forbids us to try to talk to the dead: 'Let no-one be found among you who . . . practises divination or sorcery, interprets omens, engages in witchcraft, or casts spells, or who is a medium or spiritist or who consults the dead' (Deuteronomy 18:10-11).

It may take many months or four to five years for this deep emotional wound to heal. Eventually healing comes, however. The bereaved person can carry on with life again and let the dead person rest in peace. The memories and the love are there, but the bond which kept the two people together has gradually slackened. Obviously, the degree of intensity in the mourning will be affected by the closeness of the relationship, the manner of death and the age of the deceased. But this process of grief is *essential* to healthy recovery.

Help will encourage his friend to talk, and will listen patiently even though he may have heard the anecdotes several times before. He will not urge premature acceptance or he may get an angry retort. He will keep a balance between divine comfort and essential human grief. For Christians the pain of bereavement is softened by 'the sure and certain hope of the resurrection'. For this reason sorrow and peace can co-exist. This book is not the place to examine the theological issues raised by the death of someone who appears to be an unbeliever. What a good thing *we* are not the final judge in these matters! Help's task is the same in any bereavement situation. He must just be there, listening, sharing, comforting and weeping with those who weep.

It is not always necessary to use words. Sometimes silence or touch is more eloquent. Sometimes it may be a great help to read some Scripture verses, but Help must sense whether this is the right time. Sometimes it is more appropriate to do the shopping, remove the children, or give some other practical help.

As we approach death, be it our own or that of someone we love, we usually go through some anticipatory grief. Some of this can be eased if there is an opportunity to discuss it. After all, the dying person is facing total separation from the known material world, severing relationships and making a journey into new experiences. The person left behind has to face different losses. It is a pity not to say the things that need to be said. There will not be another chance. It is also a pity not to enjoy the promises of God, *together*.

Occasionally, Help may be involved in the sad task of

trying to comfort a bereaved child. Children do suffer very greatly in this sort of loss and need to be helped to express their feelings, fears, anger and confusion. They may find it easier to do it in play and in drawings than verbally.

The reactions of bereavement are not confined to death. They can equally take place over the breakdown of a relationship, the loss of spouse or parent, removal from secure to unfamiliar surroundings, loss of a bodily function or organ, or loss of status. Help can sometimes comfort a friend more sensitively if he recognizes this.

FURTHER READING
A Grief Observed by C.S. Lewis (Faber).
Bereavement by Colin Murray Parkes (Penguin).

5

WORKING ON THE PROBLEM (II)

Failure
There are times in life when everyone has to come to terms with failure of some sort. It may be on an academic level, or a disappointment in personal relationships, or the inability of one's body to perform adequately due to some accident, illness or disability.

No-one finds failure easy: it does nothing to boost the morale. However, hard times are often the ones which teach and stretch us most, if we will allow them to do so. Failure, therefore, may be a misery at first sight, but its long-term effects can be productive. As Help tries to comfort his friend (or even to find some solace for his own wounds) he needs to think about some of the issues.

What caused this failure? It has been known for people to fail exams because they simply did not apply themselves to their work, through laziness or indiscipline! In that case the most courageous thing is to be honest and accept the unpleasant truth.

On the other hand, failure may be the result of having set an unrealistic target. In this case, Help will be asking his friend, 'Who set the target?' Who would receive the applause for success? What are the expectations of the person who set the task and the person who failed? Were they the same? When these issues have been faced honestly, the quality of the failure may then appear more clearly.

For example, some students find themselves under pressure from their school to get to university. The prestige of the school is enhanced by favourable statistics, but the pace for one particular student may be intolerable. It is very difficult to resist this pressure because anything other than higher education may seem to be 'inferior'. Is this true? The pressure may be reinforced by parents who want to draw some personal satisfaction from the fact that their offspring has achieved something which they themselves did not manage, or that their offspring is carrying on the line of clever achievement.

Perhaps the hardest pressure to resist is that which comes from within the person himself. In his inner being he feels as though he will be acceptable to others (or to himself) only if he has some piece of paper which validates him. If he can describe himself by some external role as a doctor, solicitor, teacher or architect, he will be satisfactory; but if all he has is his own inner sense of identity he is on very insecure ground. Under these circumstances, failure can lead to very acute distress. This may be the time for Help to stand alongside while his friend wrestles with some of the basic issues and grows into greater strength of personality and Christian maturity.

The growth point comes when the person concerned is prepared to acknowledge and accept his own limits and boundaries, which will include some inadequacies. It is very tempting to blame bad working conditions, incomprehensible instructors, a poor state of health, or anything which avoids facing the humiliation involved. Help is not helping his friend if he joins in this 'game'. It is hard work, emotionally, for each of us to discover the extent and the limitations of our potential. We can do so only by a process of trial and error. We have to discover whether we have ten coins or one, like the men in the parable (Luke 19:11-26). These men were each given a different number of coins and they had to go out and trade with them. They were held accountable not for the number they received but for the use they made of their potential.

It is true that within the limits of our potential we discover that we are wonderfully strengthened by Jesus Christ. 'I can do everything through him who gives me strength' (Philippians 4:13). The word 'everything' does
56

not mean that we suddenly become a superman or super-woman. It usually means that as we learn to trust the Lord and live within his will more and more, our boundaries expand. To revert to the metaphor of the men in the parable of the coins, we find that when we use our potential in conjunction with the strength and the will of God, we find that we accumulate capital gains for his kingdom.

Failure in inter-personal relationships is painful. But Help must remember that the same principles apply. The same questions need to be asked. More will be said about the area of sexual relationships in a later chapter.

The reason for some failures is difficult to find. That is especially so if, like the functioning of our body, it is beyond our conscious control. Help may find that his friend is stuck at a point of endless perplexity, continually asking 'Why?' and never finding an answer. There are many things in this life which are hard to understand and we shall never know until we reach our Celestial City.

'Why has this situation suddenly turned sour when it looked as though all was going so well?'

'Why have I been subjected to a position which is so unfair?'

Help has to distinguish between two 'Whys?': the 'Why?' which is an honest search for truth, implying willingness to face the issues and undergo a change of attitude; and the 'Why?' which is little more than an angry or anguished protest implying that the other party must do the changing. The 'Why?' of angry protest carries with it some danger that it will become a fixation, and that like a sulky child the person will concentrate on bearing a grudge and refuse to let it go. Letting go often demands humility, courage and strength.

Sometimes the search for an answer to the 'Why?' must be abandoned. The only thing to do in those circumstances is to leave the matter in the hands of God and then get on with the rest of life. Some insight may emerge much later, or when a similar pattern of failure arises again.

57

Help's immediate task, however, is to pull out whatever positive aspects there are in the situation. In the middle of failure, his friend may be able to see only the negative aspects and lose sight of the positives. Help must support his friend in thinking positively and constructively. It is very easy to slide from failure into depression. 'I have failed' gives way to 'I am a failure . . . a total failure . . . no good at anything . . . no point in trying.' These thoughts lead to a sense of hopelessness and even to the idea of suicide. The sense of hopelessness becomes engulfing so that the whole of life seems futile, meaningless and not worth the effort. Help must remember that his friend's reactions may have become distorted, just as when someone with a fever experiences a cold room as hot. In such cases Help must certainly urge his friend to seek medical help.

Throughout, however, Help must encourage his friend to cling on to the clear word of God that 'neither death nor life . . . neither the present nor the future . . . *nor anything else* . . will be able to separate us from the love of God that is in Christ Jesus our Lord' (Romans 8:38-39). Everything we are or ever shall be, and everything we have, is a gift from God. His love does not change just because we change. We are assured that when we are weak and helpless and hopeless, he comes to look for us and to carry us home like the Good Shepherd that he is – though we may be aware only of the coldness of the night, the thorn bushes, and the steepness of the path.

Furthermore, we can take heart, because not only does God forgive our mistakes, but frequently he uses them and turns them into something positive.

Drugs and alcohol

The abuse of drugs and alcohol is a social problem of major proportions today, as we know. Help must think responsibly about his own position as a Christian regarding their use, and not just drift into mindless conformity to the social pattern. I wonder whether all Christian people need to be much less casual about this whole matter.

Alcohol is a drug which produces physiological effects. If it, or any other drug, is taken as a relief from stress or tension or as a stimulant when tired or in low spirits, there are specific dangers, one of which is habit-formation. Stress, tension, tiredness and low spirits are real problems for everyone from time to time. Before we go automatically to the pub, reach for the bottle, or resort to pills of one sort or another, we need to think carefully how to deal with the root cause of the problem as responsible Christians. Is there some positive action we could take to change the pattern? What part does prayerful commitment of our daily life play in all this? In the western world we are conditioned by public opinion and the media to look for immediate relief from physical and emotional pain. Are we in danger of losing the quality of endurance and perseverance in the face of discomfort?

There is, of course, a line to be drawn between the appropriate use of drugs for medicinal purposes and their misuse. They should never be used as a stimulant, and should always be prescribed by a physician who is trained to see the physiological symptoms and effects.

While Help and his friend are discussing these things, they will also consider the amount of time and money which is being spent, bearing in mind their total commitment of everything to the Lord. Moreover, since the Christian's body and mind are a living offering to the Master in loving service, obviously he is not at liberty to subject them deliberately to disorientating experiences or influences which actively diminish his self-control.

It may seem tempting to want to understand drunkenness or a drug trip by experiencing it, but there are many occasions in life when wisdom and restraint of natural curiosity are more valuable than daring recklessness. Perhaps the life of Help's friend is rather uninteresting. This may make the prospect of exciting new experiences seem appealing. But why choose something which has so few lasting results?

A glass of wine with a meal or a quiet drink with a friend can be enjoyable as an occasional pleasure – though because the occasional pleasure can become a necessary habit, some Christians feel that even this is better avoided.

For all these practical and biblical reasons, Help will try to discourage his friend from experimenting with drugs of any sort, or becoming dependent on them without professional control.

FURTHER READING
The Abuse of Drugs by David Pott and Duncan Vere (IVP).

A defeated Christian

From time to time Help will encounter someone who is bothered about being a 'defeated Christian'. Once more, Help will remember that before he launches into the situation he must *listen*. What is his friend saying? What does this word 'defeated' signify? Is his friend using the word in a hopeless or a defiant sense?

Help will look for some clues. Does his friend mean that he feels inferior to his peer group? They all seem to be exuberant, praising and ecstatic, while he just plods on without much effervescence. Or maybe he feels that the mighty promises in God's Word just do not work for him, and he is beginning to grow despondent and doubtful. Or he may be tripped up by some 'besetting sin' which he cannot master, despite real effort and much prayer. He may be enslaved by old habits such as drug or alcohol abuse, sexual promiscuity, masturbation, or the compulsion to eat quantities of sweet foods such as chocolate and sticky buns. (It is usually 'she' who complains about this because it is so lethal for the figure!) Or he may not really know the cause. He just feels defeated. How can Help help?

If his friend feels inferior, Help must remember not to compare him with other people. Not everyone is given to noisy extroversion. His personal relationship with the Lord Jesus is better assessed on his inner willingness for loving submission and his enjoyment of being with the Lord in thought and lifestyle. If he genuinely longs for this, there is no likelihood of his being a second-class Christian. Obviously, we are all 'defeated' in the sense that we all have so far to go in knowing our dear Lord better and in opening up to ourselves all the secret recesses of our life so that we can offer them to him. (He knows them already!)

When we think about the secret recesses of our life, we may know that there are some parts which we try to hold in reserve.

'Yes, I am willing to serve the Lord – but not as a missionary.'

'Yes, I give my life and my future to him – but I do want to get married.'

We cannot have a working relationship with the Lord Jesus which has one eye on self-preservation and one on commitment. In the Christian faith, as in the marriage relationship, that attitude is a non-starter. These reservations need to be brought out and faced. We cannot live in peace with skeletons rattling in the cupboard.

There are other secret recesses which are more genuinely unknown, and they, too, need to be included. Recently I had to have a major operation. The surgeon came to my bedside, explained the reasons, procedure and results in some detail, and I listened quietly and without protest. He went away and I was left to contemplate the immediate and slightly horrific future. 'But I am a believer,' I said to myself. 'I know that all this is in the hands of my Father and there is no need to be afraid.'

An hour later, I became aware that my body was lying on the bed rigid and tense, while my mind was saying, 'There is nothing to fear.' So I had a little conversation with myself and my heavenly Father. I had genuinely not known that I was so terrified until my body sent a few important messages. We were then able to sort things out together till my attitude changed to the more realistic 'When I am afraid, I will trust in you' (Psalm 56:3).

Perhaps it is for this reason that the old Quakers used to have a time of quiet each day so that their spirit and mind and body could get together in harmony. They could then be receptive to God's word for them that day. Modern Christians still carry on the good habit, but sometimes that 'quiet' time is so laden with internal noise that there is no possibility of stilling the spirit and body. Thus, some sincere Christians become 'defeated' because they are out of step with themselves before they even approach God. This could be one reason why Help's friend finds that the great and precious promises of God do not work for him. It is no good his having a bank account if he is too busy (internally or externally) to stop and cash the cheque!

There is another possible cause of defeat. Perhaps his relationship with God has been disrupted by known and deliberate sin. God's promises apply only to people who walk with him in loving obedience. But perhaps the sin may have been committed in ignorance (which does not make it any less of a sin!). It is important therefore to get to know the Bible by very frequent reading and memorizing, so that we are not ignorant of the way God wants us to live. I say 'memorizing' because the Holy Spirit can bring to our mind for immediate use only that which is already there. Also, a day may come when we no longer have free access to the written Word of God.

If Help's friend is troubled by some habit which he cannot control, Help will try to distinguish between things that differ. Some old habits can be broken by the application of a little will-power, self-discipline and common sense. There is no need for us to wring our hands helplessly as though we were hostages to fate. Help can strengthen his friend's resolve, support and encourage him, and perhaps help him to replace the undesirable activity with something more positive and wholesome. This will assist his friend to accomplish something which would be much more difficult to achieve by himself.

Perhaps the problem is not so much the habit itself as the

guilt and misery associated with it. The need for urgent physical relief of sexual tension in masturbation need not necessarily have anything to do with our relationship with God. Only if it becomes fixated at an auto-erotic level is it potentially damaging to relationships. The need to eat as a way of comforting an inner emptiness is not in itself wrong. It makes great sense to a hungry psyche. So it is important to discover wherein lies the guilt and the awful feeling of failure about constant breaking of renewed intentions. Is it true guilt or false guilt? Help, however, may find himself out of his depth here. If so, he would be wise to suggest that his friend looked for more experienced and professional help.

If Help's friend has a hopeless, general, non-specific sense of being 'a defeated Chritian', it may sometimes indicate an underlying depression. Help should be on the watch for this and take steps to help his friend with the total situation, not just one aspect of it.

Help must hold at the centre of his thinking the fact that God is sovereign in the lives of his people. He must encourage his friends in the solid knowledge that God is not dead. He is always at work in the details of our lives. The Bible is shot through from beginning to end with this, both in the stories and in the direct teaching. This foundation belief, backed by experience, will affect both behaviour and feelings. It leaves little room for a Christian to be seriously defeated on a permanent basis.

FURTHER READING
Spiritual Dryness by Walter Trobish (IVP).

Parents

Parents can be a fearful problem, but they can also be very good friends. Growing up is a difficult business. It is all about separating emotionally from parents and acquiring one's own identity. Birth is the first painful stage of a frequently painful process. The new baby is out on its own in the physical world, dramatically a separate person, though utterly helpless, dependent and vulnerable.

As he grows within his family the child increasingly understands the emotional demands which the members make on each other. He may learn that if he is good his parents are nice to him, and if he is naughty they seem to withdraw their love. He may see that his mother cannot resist tears and so he may begin to realize that he can get his own way by crying. He may learn that his parents are trustworthy and that it is safe to rely on what they say. These, and hundreds of unspoken messages, are repeated daily, and so he forms his own view of himself, of people who have power over him, and of the various ways in which people get what they want.

Going to school is the next important separation experience. Now there are other people who have power and who can exert pressures and require standards. Most parents experience at least a twinge of emotional discomfort when little Johnny comes home from school saying, 'But *teacher* says . . .', and the parents realize that they are no longer the final authority. Separation is an experience felt by parents as well as children.

The gap is reinforced heavily again at adolescence. This is a notoriously troublesome time because the adolescent now has more independence with which to back up his position. He wants to establish that he is an individual person in his own right. This may seem to involve total abandonment of parental standards and values. It is very painful for parents to stand by quietly and watch their careful 'foundation-building' being turned upside down. A very great degree of trust, both in God and in their offspring, is required of parents at such a time, and sometimes the requirement is too great. It is hard for younger people to understand this.

At the same time it is essential for the young to acquire their own separate identity. Certainly the shape of the identity they acquire will be related to the atmosphere in the parental home, but it must be a *separate* identity. A certain amount of struggle and conflict is almost inevitable. The very struggle assists the development of emotional muscle.

Help may easily find himself involved with a friend whose parents are 'a problem'. He may need to discover whether it is the parents, or his friend – or both – who are the problem! He will certainly have to ask what the struggle is about. Who is afraid of losing what? Is that a realistic fear? Is each party in the struggle really trying to see the other's viewpoint as well as his own? I think it is often difficult to help one's peers with this problem. It may be that Help has not resolved his own position satisfactorily. In that case it is difficult to be objective. It may be more appropriate to seek help from an experienced older person who can see the conflict more dispassionately.

Philip came from a staunch Christian family where almost every activity was focused round the church. His father was a lay reader and his mother the leader of the women's fellowship – both fairly powerful people. They forged ahead militantly and it was taken as read that Philip would follow. His questionings and personal search for truth were regarded as rebellion and lack of faith, and a lesser fellow might have taken the line of least resistance. However, he was determined. He was sad to see the way they were hurt, and he wished they could accept that he could not be a pale reflection of them. He thought they were fearfully narrow-minded, and he wanted to broaden his experience of life. Sometimes he was not as tactful as he could have been: both Philip and his parents were very forthright people. Help had to stand by trying to persuade him to quieten his louder outbursts and holding the balance between Philip and his parents.

Martin, by contrast, could not maintain the struggle. He found his parents so possessive that his way of handling the problem was to sever connections, which was a pity, and not really necessary. But he felt he could not stand the emotional strain of having them breathing down his neck. He preferred not to go home on vacations. The atmosphere was too tense and he flew off the handle too easily when he was provoked. Help had to talk with Martin about his unrealistic fears that his parents could really stop him from growing. He tried to help Martin to be firm and yet considerate.

Kate was always worried about her parents. They had a very poor relationship with each other and Kate was sure a divorce would come one day. She felt responsible for them and anxious to do something to improve matters. It was very hard work for Kate to withdraw some of her own emotional dependency on her parents and to realize that she was *not* responsible for them, nor had she any direct ability to improve their relationship. Only as Help encouraged her to take a few emotional steps away from them could she offer both of them a degree of understanding which was free from overtones of anxiety and demand.

Anne had a lovely home, though. Her parents were so good and kind and she was always happiest when she was with them. She was hoping she might marry soon so that she could set up her own home, which would be like her parents'. The unaccountable depression which always seemed to be in the background was a constant mystery. Her mother, anxious to help, was subtly and unconsciously reinforcing Anne's dependence by protectiveness and fussing. Slowly and painfully Anne began to see that she was so safe and comfortable with her parents that she was afraid to separate emotionally. She could separate geographically, but always *felt* a part of them. She hated the thought of not knowing what they were thinking or doing. She was afraid she would disintegrate if she had to stand alone emotionally, and the fear of trying was considerable. Help had a tough job in trying to stand alongside because Anne was not all sure that she wanted things to change.

All families have invisible emotional pushes and pulls which operate between the various members. Each person influences the others in some way. When one person within the family network begins to change his position, this inevitably affects the other members. If the effects are uncomfortable, pressure may be exerted to push him back into the previous position. So Help must encourage his friend to ask himself *why* he wants to change position. Is it essential? How is it going to impinge on the others? What is it going to achieve? What is the new pattern intended to be? Is he doing it in the most helpful way?

Although change is usually uncomfortable, it is important to cause as little deliberate distress as possible. It is desirable to be open and communicate honestly with the people who will be affected, and make a genuine effort to understand their thoughts. This is easier said than done. But a belligerent and offensive stance is bound to create tension. If a change *has* to be made, let it be done courteously and firmly, remembering that God's Word says we must honour and respect our parents (Exodus 20:12; Ephesians 6:1-3).

Growing up within a family means that the children are moving towards relating to their parents as independent adults, financially, socially and emotionally. The degrees of dependence will be very different, and so the quality of the relationship will be different. But the degree of love and concern need not change.

6

SEXUAL RELATIONSHIPS (1)

(Welcome to those who have just joined us – though you should really start at the beginning, if you want to be a well-founded and really useful Help!)

The problem of sexual relationships
Perhaps the problem of sexual relationships is the most popular of them all! I wonder how many man- or woman-hours have been spent since the beginning of the human race on this fascinating and excruciating bitter-sweet subject! Surely, the problems, pains, joys and uncertainties of male–female relationships provide as much confirmation of God's goodness, and also of our fallenness, as we are ever likely to need.

It is a subject of fundamental importance to everyone. Our sexual gender is basic to the whole composition of our individual personality. There are the inbuilt emotional and physical drives and needs, to say nothing of the cultural expectations of society. The idea that men and women are equal is open to much misinterpretation. Of course they are equal in the sight of God and in human dignity and value, and should not be treated otherwise. The differences are fundamental, however, and therein lies the strength of the sexual tension. Anatomically, there are both similarities and complete and complementary differences. There are also psychological similarities and differences. The difference within equality can be a delight and enrichment, if understood properly. The confusions and struggles which characterize society (and many Christians) in their sexual behaviour are basically about failure to grasp the details of this general fact.

Perhaps it will be helpful briefly to define my terms. I use the word 'sex' to refer to purely physical attributes or activities. The word 'sexuality', on the other hand, includes much wider concepts such as 'Who am I?', 'How do I express my inner creative drives?' (since sex, sexuality and creation are inalienably linked), and 'How do I see myself in relation to men, and in relation to women?' Thus 'sexuality' is a very comprehensive and personal word.

Help needs to bear in mind a basic generalization, namely, that on the whole it is the nature of men to be interested in objective ideas, theories, technology, reason and science; and on the whole, it is the nature of women to be interested in subjective feelings, relationships, emotions and inner being. Of course, there is no sharp division. Each of us is bisexual with a strong bias towards masculinity or femininity.

A grasp of this essential difference will go some way to explaining the tension. Why can a man walk away relatively unscathed, leaving a girl deeply hurt? Why is a girl concerned about the quality and nature of their relationship, while a man may take it more for granted? Why can many women be thinking of four things at once, whereas many men can deal with only one thing at a time? Why does a woman often know things before they have been specified, while a man cannot account for it logically? It is all in 'the nature of the beast'. A considerable degree of unhappiness and stress can be alleviated if Help has a clear understanding of this.

Paul Tournier has some helpful things to say about it in his book *The Gift of Feeling*. He equates the masculine principle with *power*, and the feminine principle with *person*. Each has something to contribute to the other.

The student comes up to university or college and all the world is there – hundreds of new faces, male and female. Freedom is relatively unrestricted and the choice is wide. But the student brings with him a whole network of social and emotional experiences which colour his thinking. She may have been at a single-sex school; he may have been the only boy among a family of girls, or one of a family of boys with no sisters. She may have watched all her friends pairing off at school, and now this is *her* big chance. So not only is the field wide, but the expectations and hesitations are wide as well. Student years are the time for fun, but at the back of it is the dreadful spectre of the possibility of ending up single.

As time goes on things change. Our new Christian student has made many friends and is being drawn more seriously to one special person. 'Is this the "right" person for me?' It is important to be sure. Much earnest prayer and discussion take place. How can one *know*?

There are some broad guidelines which it might be useful to consider, and Help needs to know them as part of his helping equipment. Probably Help himself is also wrestling with some of these issues.

The physical pull
If this relationship is largely dominated by physical excitement and stimulation, there is a great possibility that it will be only a transient phase. Our 'chemical reactions' can be so overpowering that they overcome our rational judgment and make everything seem idyllic. But *chemical reactions are not an infallible guide.* The trouble about being 'turned on' in this way is that the thrills of embrace and the emotional warmth seem almost sufficient in themselves. The physical satisfaction is often far more intense than the quality of this relationship. A deep personal trust is not necessarily being established. Physical stimulation *is* very important and its satisfactions can last a long time, but unless they are accompanied by a proved and deepening personal relationship they will eventually fizzle out.

It is quite hard to be a Help in this situation. The overwhelming force of the emotional flow will probably make any rational discussion useless. Only in retrospect does reason come into its own. Perhaps the best thing for the people concerned is to refrain from making any major and serious decisions like marriage or deep commitment during such a time. Not a few people find themselves married, knowing everything about each other's bodies and very little about each other as people. Then the scene is set for disaster and much personal pain.

The current climate of opinion which we see all around us is that sexual happiness and achievement are the ideal goal. It is very tempting to envy people who are having a lively sex life. We all have our own very strong physical needs. There is also the awful feeling of being out of step and peculiar if we are on our own. Society is geared to couples and regards them as the norm. That, in itself, is enough to make us embark on a desperate search to find a partner. Almost any partner may seem better than none.

Some people need, as a reassurance, the vibrant physical sexual responses which are evoked in them. They are not sure that they do much else well, but at least this is all right – and so sexual activity acquires a special and urgent significance. If the partner who has been providing the stimulation disappears, the resultant pain can be twofold – loss of a friend and loss of the stimulation. When physical stimulation is important for its own sake, people can easily become promiscuous, because it is the sensation and not the partner *as a person* that really matters.

Christian people have strong, normal, sexual desires, and sometimes need inner reassurance. We also respond in the same ways as everyone else to sexual stimulation and closeness. We need to think very carefully about appropriate attitudes for a Christian person to his own sexual needs and to his sexuality.

FURTHER READING
Eros Defiled by John White (IVP), ch. 3: 'Your urges and how you experience them'.

The wholeness of love
What of the situation where there is a 'loving relationship'

in addition to chemical reactions?

This poor old word 'love' has been so overworked that we now have to distinguish between the various meanings it has acquired. Let us be quite clear that 'love' and 'sex' are not synonymous. Sex is merely an activity common to humans and animals, and it is often no more connected with love than is washing one's face.

Hopping into bed as the conclusion of a night out is not necessarily anything to do with love. It is often merely the meeting of a physical need or the expected behavioural response. When it is over it is relatively meaningless. Alternatively it may stir up feelings which are then left floating. The discomfort of unattached emotional arousal will probably impel the person to search around for someone else to whom to attach it, if the original source is not available. Someone who is trying to satisfy an unmet emotional need can become 'addicted' to sex in the same way as he can be hooked on drugs or alcohol.

Sexual behaviour and personhood are inextricably connected. In our schizoid generation people are in the habit of splitting their bodily behaviour from their essential spirit. But this is a costly thing to do. Sexual experience is designed to carry with it deep affirmation of the person of one's partner and of oneself. If this does not happen, a vital part of one's total personality is cut off, deprived, or underdeveloped. Christian people need to state this fact repeatedly in an age when sex is frequently misused.

Perhaps I should spell it out in more detail so that Help can find his own way and also help others through the maze.

Human beings are created as a whole entity, each part dependent on and reflecting other parts. We are not designed to function as a collection of disconnected, assorted parts tied up in a bag (a body). When someone's spirit is filled with a sense of well-being, his body is relaxed and moves gracefully, his skin is clear and his eyes alive. This person radiates vitality: he has a quality of openness which enables him to relate warmly and in depth with other people. They feel valued by him and enjoy being with him. Conversely, when the inner spirit experiences deprivation and emptiness and a sense of worthlessness, the body reflects the inner pain by becoming lifeless, awkward and stiff, skin and eyes grow dull, and psychosomatic symptoms may appear. There is a closed quality about that person which keeps others at a distance; people feel ill at ease with him because he takes little interest in them.

In an ideal situation, there is a continuity of character from the inside to the outside. As an onion has many layers, all sharing the same characteristics, so the outward expression of someone's personality can be a true indication of his inner essence. A superficial acquaintance would provide knowledge which would be in keeping with subsequent discoveries at a deeper level.

We do not live in an ideal situation, however, and the image of wholeness and consistency reflecting God's character has been damaged. Many of us have been emotionally hurt along the way, and we attempt to comfort and heal those inner wounds through the experiences which our body can give us.

Geoffrey was such a person. He had never been sure that he was loved. He never remembered any physical affection from his parents. Then Barbara came into his life. She also had a great deal of insecurity and in no time they found themselves clinging to, and needing, each other. At weekends they slept in the same bed. They greatly appreciated the closeness and warmth of each other's bodies. They were not specially interested in intercourse; it was so good to find the other still there, and smiling, in the morning. It seemed to be such a healing and gratifying experience.

That physical closeness is the basis on which the mother-infant relationship rests. Our earliest experiences as infants are related to the satisfactions we received from the sight, smell and closeness of our mothers' bodies. It spells security, reliability, continuity, assurance, care, and all the things which we understand as love. If the experiences in early childhood were seriously defective, those infant needs still remain unmet. They will become activated by the sight, sound and smell of another person in later life, but it is inappropriate for adults to be fixated at an infantile level of behaviour. Nevertheless, many needy people do behave in this way. The trouble with this is that it is not the basis for an adult-to-adult relationship. Although Geoffrey and Barbara had 'found' each other and consoled each other significantly, they were both still lost in the wood and their mutual comfort was not finding the way out for them.

Help would be in a dilemma in this circumstance. It might appear monstrous to encourage these two to alter the behaviour through which at last some nourishment has come to them. But it is essential for Help to remember, and to remind Geoffrey and Barbara, they are not infants in *every* sense. They must not allow immediate gratification to blind them to the wider issues of relationship. Very often in situations like this, as time passes, so does the immediacy of the comfort. And then the hurt starts all over again, with no real progress being made. As Help understands more of his friends' needs he will remind Geoffrey and Barbara that growth in the knowledge and love of God means that they put away childish things. 'When I was a child, I talked like a child, I thought like a child, I reasoned like a child. When I became a man, I put childish ways behind me' (1 Corinthians 13:11). Adult love no longer needs gratification on an infantile level. It is about giving as well as receiving. It is able to include such concepts as God's purposes and his wholeness (which also include certain restraints). The adult approach is to ask, 'What is God's will in this, and does what I am doing reflect his intentions?' – not 'What is *my* will in this situation?'

One of the ways in which we defend ourselves against pain is to split that bit off, push it out and remove it; but then we are no longer consistent from inside to outside. Jean gives us an example of this. Having given herself in a sexual relationship which failed, she hardened herself a bit. Next

74

time, she will keep something in reserve, so that if it goes wrong it will not matter so much. So Jean deliberately breaks her 'inner-to-outer continuity' as a means of self-preservation, and becomes a less complete person as a result.

In his book *Eros Defiled*, John White says: 'Erotic pleasure is the most superficial benefit of sex. It is a delight but only the delight of a moment. The bodily exposure that arouses and accompanies it can be both profoundly symbolic and powerfully healing. It symbolizes the uncovering of our inner selves, our deepest fears and yearnings. As I look tenderly on the body of another, as I experience what it is to feel the tenderness of another's caresses and the delight of knowing I am loved as well as loving, it seems momentarily impossible to separate myself from my body. So much am I a bodily creature that the one who accepts my body, caresses also with tenderness my innermost being. Or so at times it seems.'

But Dr White also points out: 'A human encounter is fraught with fear that the other will reject and despise me when he discovers what I (really) am. I am torn between the yearning to expose myself and the fear of shame and of another's scorn. I long to cast aside every shred that covers me and be known and loved for my naked self. Yet though I am tired of the many masks I hide behind, the disguises with which I confront the world I live in; though they are burdensome and heavy, concealing the deformities and weaknesses I hate and fear – if I strip them from me, how terrible is the risk I run!'

Help's goal is not simply to press a negative viewpoint about abstaining from fornication, but rather to be in constant pursuit of personal growth and clearer 'continuity'. When a person experiences one dimension alone of his person-hood, such as the physical or the intellectual, he is diminishing himself. If there is pressure to experience physical pleasure at the expense of reason, or intellect at the expense of feelings, there is discontinuity and the person's full potential is stunted. With regard to interpersonal relationships, the aim is to develop the full potential of one's own being whilst encouraging the wholeness and 'continuity' of the other person.

This involves movement towards increased sensitivity and awareness, by honesty and openness, integration of intellect and emotion, often with a resulting sense of increased physical well-being. This sort of relationship leads to increased understanding of our own inner self and thus enables us to be more affirming to other people. No-one can reach out whole-heartedly to other people if he himself is twisted up inside.

Psychiatrist Jack Dominian describes it this way: 'The most conducive conditions for growth are *relationships* of *permanency, continuity, reliability* and *predictability* which allow the partners to understand each other and to act as facilitating agents, bringing to the fore each other's talents, and helping to formulate clearly that which is latent and confused within . . . reinforcing initiative, encouraging experimentation, providing succour at times of pain, failure and despair, helping us to face the dark side of ourselves.'

Relationships of fornication or adultery do not provide this permanent undergirding of stability. Of course, marriage in itself does not guarantee quality. It is the 100% commitment to deepening the relationship that is essential for producing quality. That, of necessity, includes permanence.

This is the reason why God has so much to say about sexual behaviour in the Bible. For instance: 'It is God's will that you should be holy [whole]; that you should avoid sexual immorality; that each of you should learn to control his own body in a way that is holy and honourable, not in passionate lust like the heathen, who do not know God; and that in this matter no-one should wrong his brother or take advantage of him' (1 Thessalonians 4:3-6).

Falling in love

We ought to think about the variations on the theme of 'being in love'. Franz Schubert is alleged to have been very much in love with his pupil, the young Countess Caroline Esterhazy. He told her that all his musical outpourings were dedicated to her. History gives us no evidence, however, that he made any solid attempt to translate this into a real encounter of two people.

I remember Jane, a girl who doted on a graduate research student at the same university. She would wait around so that she could 'accidentally' meet him; she would treasure up any note or conversation they exchanged, and had succeeded in persuading herself that there was a secret liaison going on between them. It had to be secret, she said. It would not do for it to be public, because he was a senior person in the student hierarchy and in the Christian Union.

Although there was no tangible sign of there being a reciprocated relationship as far as other people could notice, Jane went on with this for more than a year. In many ways she was a sensible, intelligent girl, but on this point she seemed to be labouring under a delusion. Nothing ever came of this secret 'love', except that she had successfully prevented herself from being attracted to any of the other available men. Although she was attractive and wanted a loving relationship with a man, she had become 'stuck' emotionally and could not engage in something which might have exposed her to the realities of an adult-to-adult encounter. She had a great investment in 'worshipping from afar', and Jane needed skilled help in enabling her to work through the blockage which she saw as 'being in love'.

Jane had a friend, Hazel, who tried to be a Help to her. Hazel reminded her frequently of the unreality of the situation, and tried to persuade Jane to give up the useless dream, but to no avail. No amount of rational argument had any lasting effect on Jane. Hazel could do no more, and had to leave the problem. Wisely, she recognized that this was something beyond her competence.

77

Life in the fantasy world of being in love can be made so exciting and painless that there is no need to get to grips with the difficulties of the real world. The danger of the fantasy world is that it eliminates the need to grow by grappling with reality.

Literature is full of eloquent descriptions about what happens when people are in love. Things happen which to a dispassionate spectator are quite incredible. John describes Mary in terms which are often a bit unrealistic, making 'woeful ballads to his mistress' eyebrow'; Susan's whole life has taken on a new vivacity since she met Robert. Something very powerful is taking place which can be positive, fulfilling and enriching. Being 'in love', however, is only part of the story and is not in itself a good ground for making life-long promises.

Falling in love is one way of describing a projection. We make up our own picture of the ideal person, put that image on to someone else, and then proceed to treat that person as though he did actually possess the qualities with which we have invested him.

There is a description of this in that old-fashioned book called the Bible. In the book of Isaiah the prophet describes people who had cut down trees which had been growing in the forest (Isaiah 44:14-20). They used some of the wood as fuel for heating and cooking. The rest they carved into some shape which appealed to them. They then worshipped it, saying, 'Save me; you are my god.' They did not stop to think that *they* had made this idol and it was powerless of itself. They had invested a piece of wood with superhuman qualities, and in the very nature of things it could only disappoint their expectations.

'Projection', or putting our own expectations on to someone else, is a human device as old as the hills. There is bound to be some involuntary element of projection in almost every relationship we make. In the matter of being 'in love', all these splendid projections of strength, gentleness, brilliance, beauty, generosity, or whatever else, are very easy to

78

worship. They feel 'so right' when they have been attached to someone else. If they happen to be there in reality, our joy is complete. If they are not there, we may take recourse to another device and deny their absence: 'You don't understand John'; 'I'm sure Mary will change'; 'He's not like that when he's with me'. The language of 'in-love' is to a large extent 'How can you meet my needs?'; 'I want you to turn me on'; 'While you do these things for me I am filled with delight.' (But what will happen when you don't, can't or won't do it any longer?)

Staying in love
Falling in love is easy but staying in love is a skill and an art which is very hard work and needs much practice and patience. It is so easy to love someone who comes up to one's 'ideal', but what will happen when the unexpected realities begin to emerge – when there are real differences, disappointments, nasty rough edges which hurt? What when this god or goddess begins to reveal feet of clay? Then comes the test. At that point, 'being in love' will begin to change to 'loving', which acknowledges the good and the bad. If not, the relationship will begin to disintegrate, sometimes with much heartache.

Colin and Helen were superficially happy together, but within certain limits. If Colin was ever challenged seriously about something he really wanted, he would go into a furious rage, hammering the furniture with his fists and shouting. People soon learnt to steer clear of the danger zone. By this emotional blackmail Colin had his way about everything that was significant to him. Helen dared not confront him; she had not dealt with the situation when it first arose in their relationship, and now, after all these years, it was virtually too difficult. So she took the line of least resistance. Their 'love' included a big element of collusion, which was unhealthy for both of them and which decreased the quality of their relationship as time went by.

Helen asked her Help about this, but it was a delicate

situation. Help had, first, to try and help Helen face her own reluctance to stand up to Colin's outbursts. Why was she so afraid of conflict and aggression? Had she ever learnt how to handle her own or other people's anger? What did she fear, and was it a realistic fear? What was her contribution to this collusion?

In response to leading questions, Helen was able to reflect that she had always been afraid of her father's temper and so had got used to avoiding trouble. She had tried to keep her feelings under control because she 'didn't know what would happen' if she gave vent to them. So she had had no experience of any constructive ways of using these feelings. She had just squashed them. And now she was transferring this habit to her relationship with Colin. Help had to help Helen think her way into the situation and discover what she really wanted, whether she could change the *status quo,* and how she herself had to stand on her own feet more in order to help Colin to grow up a bit.

Colin was not asking for help. Men often find it more difficult to ask, but in any case, Colin did not see himself as having a problem – until he found that Helen was changing slightly and he could not shout his way to victory quite so easily. They were able, eventually, to tolerate the discomfort of the fairly radical changes that they both had to make in their attitudes to themselves and each other. Help could only be encouraging and supportive. Colin and Helen had to do their own hard work themselves.

We have the old saying that love is blind, but in fact genuine love is not blind. Love sees with clearer penetration than any other emotion, but love is willing to face the truth, accept it, and attempt to deal with the situation in whatever way is tolerable, constructive and gentle. Love is prepared to *look* at the idol's feet and see whether or not they are made of clay. Love is prepared to ask searching questions and not to tolerate less than the highest good for the object of its love. Love is, to a large extent, a matter of will, which acknowledges the clay feet as well as the strengths.

What a statement about a mature personality! In modern parlance we might say that love is a relationship in which there is no subtle manipulation, no using the other person to enable me to maintain my chosen position of dependence, independence or whatever makes me feel safe.

Love allows the other person to go free. Perhaps that is the hardest saying of all. The innate selfishness of each of us instinctively wants to put chains around some valued person to keep him or her for ourselves. Will his/her freedom threaten me? The ability to allow this freedom to someone implies a deep level of trust, commitment, personal integration and maturity.

Love's conflicts

What does love do when it sees some inconsistency or weakness in the other person? Love searches its own heart first. It is so much easier to blame the other for being wrong than to see how I may have contributed to that wrong. It is a much easier way out to say 'You are wrong' than to admit 'I am sorry'. Love will try, with great sensitivity, courage and honesty, to understand what this 'wrong' is all about and why it occurs. It will do everything in its power to promote a sense of trust and emotional security, without destructive criticism – but it will not be afraid of constructive conflict which can often deepen understanding. Such conflict, which leads to fuller trust and commitment and new vistas of love, is an aspect of the art and skill of loving; but it does require courage and commitment to the relationship by both people. Fortunately Colin and Helen had this courage and commitment to each other, which helped them to face up to themselves and what was happening in their relationship.

All this highlights the significance of the words in 1 Corinthians 13:4-8a (RSV), about the quality of love and its relationship to personal maturity. 'Love is patient and kind; love is not jealous or boastful; it is not arrogant or rude. Love does not insist on its own way; it is not irritable or resentful; it does not rejoice at wrong, but rejoices in the right. Love

81

bears all things, believes all things, hopes all things, endures all things. Love never ends.'

All this also highlights the language of sex. Words are always reinforced with physical gestures, looks, attitudes and approaches. Sexual intercourse (unless it is purely equated with animal behaviour) is intended to confirm the message 'I am giving my inner being to you in trust' or 'I love you dearly' or 'thank-you' or 'You are forgiven' – and a thousand other messages.

There is a plain, though different, parallel in the love of the Lord for his people when he gave them the ultimate proof of his love, saying, 'This is my body.' The intention was that we should feed on him in our hearts and be nourished into human and spiritual maturity by the significance of his permanent and total dedication to us. We receive his love with thanksgiving, but the very receiving of it implies a response of our love. Does this analogy seem shocking? In this picture-language God highlights his love and commitment to us human beings. It stands in stark contrast to our human emotional and sexual relationships when, as so frequently, we use them for personal gratification with little long-term commitment.

Love and holiness
In the light of this, casual sex (although that phrase is a contradiction in terms), or sex which does not imply commitment and permanence, can be seen for what it is. There are many persuasive arguments for it, however.

'Everyone does it';

'As long as no-one gets hurt it's all right' (though often someone does get hurt in the end);

'I shall lose him if I don't give in' (emotional blackmail?);

'I shall be thought wet if I have no experience';

'He says that if I love him I ought to be willing to prove it' – thus runs the 'reasoning'.

For the Christian, the most convincing reasoning comes from the wisdom of the Word of God. When the children of

Israel were about to enter their new country of Canaan, the Lord told them clearly through Moses that the people in the nations all round them would behave in ways which were *not appropriate for the people of God.* 'You must not do as they do . . . Be holy because I, the Lord your God, am holy' (Leviticus 18:3; 19:2). This sort of warning was repeated again and again during their subsequent history (2 Kings 17:15 *etc.*). One of the most frequent objections of the Lord God, the Holy One of Israel, to the behaviour of the pagan people in surrounding nations, was their indiscriminate sexual behaviour.

Then again, the Lord Jesus Christ himself in the Sermon on the Mount told his would-be followers repeatedly not to take their standards from the surrounding peoples. 'Do not be like them' (Matthew 6:8); 'Be perfect... as your heavenly Father is perfect' (Matthew 5:48). At the conclusion of, and integral to, his monumental treatise on the great truths of our faith, Paul says, 'Therefore... in view of God's mercy... do not conform any longer to the pattern of this world, but be transformed by the renewing of your mind' (Romans 12:1-2). This principle refers to standards of sexual behaviour and also to materialistic attitudes and the whole of the Christian's orientation in this world.

One of the clearest ways of witness to the love of the Lord for us and our responsive love for him in today's world is that we take his standards seriously. His standards are 'continuity from inner to outer', truth, purity, integrity and honour. They also include respect for other people's spirits and bodies at a very deep level.

FURTHER READING
Sex in the Real World by Lewis Smedes (Lion).
Growing into Love and *Two Into One?* by Joyce Huggett (IVP).
The Growth of Love and Sex by Jack Dominian (Darton, Longman and Todd).

SEXUAL RELATIONSHIPS (II)

A previous generation of Christians imposed external controls on sexual excitement by 'the six-inch rule': there was always to be a gap of at least six inches between you and someone of the opposite sex. This has since attracted much ridicule, and indeed it is healthier to look for internal controls than for rules imposed from outside. A parent is always glad when he realizes that his son is thinking, 'I will not resort to lying because that diminishes me as a person', rather than 'Father says it is wrong to tell lies'. There are times in this life, however, when internal controls are under very hard pressure from conflicting desires. Then we need some reinforcement from outside to enable us to keep God's standards of internal and external holiness (wholeness). We should also remember in our relationships never to push someone else beyond the boundaries they can tolerate. It seems trite, but may be helpful, to remind ourselves that each little step in physical intimacy impels us on towards the next. It is hard to go back. We can only go forward. Hair-raising adventures in the first relationship become all part of the scene in the second. So, if we put our hand in the fire, there is not much point in subsequently whining to God, 'Why did you let me get burnt?' It is a source of great consolation that God does help us so gently with the results of so much of our own foolishness.

Living together
One of the standards of this world which exerts pressure on the Christian is the concept of 'freedom'. People do not want the restrictions and responsibilities of marriage, but they do want the privileges and joys of an intimate relation-

ship. They want freedom. Their resolution of this dilemma is to live with a partner without the marriage covenant. Also, it makes economic sense in some cases. This 'freedom' often boils down to meaning that I want to do what I want to do, when and where I want to do it, without much consideration about how that impinges on anyone else. It's my life and I shall decide how I live it, they say. But 'freedom' is not the same as 'unaccountability'.

The crucial issue here is about commitment: permanent commitment. The refusal to face commitment seems to permeate all life very deeply so it is no surprise that sexual relationships are included. Underneath all the reasoning lies the proviso, 'I will stick with it if it works out comfortably, but if things get rough, I reserve the right to withdraw.' Or as it has been expressed elsewhere, 'I love you; I love you; I love you, and I'll see you on Friday if it isn't raining.'

There is a certain limited honesty in people who are not prepared to sink everything in the promise 'for better for worse, for richer for poorer, in sickness and in health ... till death us do part'. It is true that many a relationship that went well till marriage hits hard times after that step has been taken. The closure of the escape-hatches seems to heighten anxiety and tension. The problems involved in living together may have been worked out reasonably well, but marriage presents a different set of problems. The resolution of the first set does not guarantee the resolution of the second set.

Elizabeth and Jane had been friends since they met as students. During that period Jane had formed a fairly intense relationship with Graham and after several months they decided to move in together. Elizabeth and Jane had discussed it at length, and Elizabeth had asked Jane about the future of this relationship. She had asked why, if they loved each other enough to make a 60% commitment to each other, did they stop short of 100%?

Jane had been annoyed and said it didn't feel like that. She had been very confident that they would marry one day. They were very much in love, wanted to share their lives with each other and didn't need a piece of paper to prove it. In the unlikely event of it not working out, they could part company. There would be no harm done and, moreover, there would not be all the ugliness of a divorce and that sort of thing.

Graham and Jane had wanted it to be a fairly secret arrangement, but it was not the sort of arrangement that could stay secret for long. People began to ask questions. But it seemed to work well. Elizabeth heard Jane saying how wonderful it all was and gradually became convinced that her own misgivings about it must have been wrong. Eventually the two girls began to go their separate ways.

Unexpectedly, they met again two years later and Elizabeth made some enquiries about Graham. Jane was particularly rude in her reply and Elizabeth wondered what to do. Obviously the Graham episode was over. Elizabeth wanted to help Jane in her angry pain, but each time she made an overture Jane would almost scream at her to get out. It seemed impossible for Elizabeth to say the right thing. It had not occurred to either Elizabeth or Jane that the break-up of any intense relationship is similar to bereavement or a divorce. Jane was still in emotional mourning, and without much supportive help because of the nature of her relationship with Graham.

Elizabeth nevertheless kept in touch, gently and without probing, and eventually Jane began to say how awful the pain of breaking up had been. She had been, and still was, very fond of Graham. He had been of her, and probably still was in a way. She had really thought this relationship would work out and be permanent. But Graham had an eye on his career. Jane was never sure what he was going to do or where he would be and whether she fitted in to this picture. That made her feel insecure. She realized afterwards, too, that when they went out together he always introduced her as 'Jane'. 'Well, there are thousands of Janes about, aren't there? I had no name and no status and it made me feel anonymous and impersonal. At first I didn't mind, but gradually I grew to feel resentful. I did the same to him, of course.'

The confusion of an ill-defined relationship had had a strangely undermining effect on her personally and in her relations with other people. It had begun to seem as though Graham, although he said he loved her, was really biding his time until he was ready to move on to the next stage of his life. In the end, all these unresolved frustrations made them fractious with each other, and Jane began to realize that she was losing an excellent boyfriend because she was living with him. The thought of suicide had crossed her mind, but really that wasn't her style and she was sensible enough to know that emotional blackmail would only make matters worse.

Elizabeth listened to all this and could feel her friend's grief, loneliness and confusion. She did not know what to say. Jane's jibe was true – Elizabeth didn't know what it felt like. So she sat quietly, without condemning or criticizing, but trying to make it obvious that she cared and would go on caring. She wished in vain that there were some easy answer. She prayed, of course, but Jane did not feel much like praying. Elizabeth felt she had been a poor Help. She asked herself if she could have done more. She learnt from this, however, something about the cost of standing alongside and helping her friend to struggle painfully on to sound ground. There was little more she could have done. The important thing was to *be there* when she was needed.

Jane had to struggle with her hurt emotions, and also to come to the point of acknowledging that God's Word is ultimately for our health and protection, not to spoil our fun. God loves us. He is on our side. He is not some far off tyrannical despot who has no idea what our life is like. The concept of living together without both private and public declaration of permanence (or, come to that, marriage with the open option of divorce) is anti-Christian, however right it may feel. God is totally committed to us in love regardless of our ups and downs. His aim is our constant growth on every level towards continuity, maturity and completeness. This cannot be done if some parts are held back in reserve, or if we persist in living counter to his standards of holiness. If we are Christians we cannot adopt an alternative system which disobeys the Lord and so very often ends in hurt, disillusionment and discontinuity.

Christians are, of course, confronted with the desire to have intercourse outside of marriage. They, too, sometimes think about the possibility of living together before marriage. There are many pros and cons, but the final test is, 'What is the word of God about this?' We saw in the last chapter that God's Word encourages us to be holy as he is holy. Are we measuring our standards by those of the heathen around us who do not know God, or are we wanting to walk before our loving Lord in willing obedience, even if it is sometimes hard? Our *body* is the temple of the Holy Spirit; we are not our own, to please ourselves, but we have been bought with a price – the death of Jesus Christ. So Paul enjoins us to flee from sexual immorality and to honour God with our bodies (1 Corinthians 6:18-20).

In his graphic exposition of the apocalyptic symbolism in the book of Revelation, *I Saw Heaven Opened*, Michael Wilcock paints a picture of the final consummation of glory when 'the marriage of the Lamb' takes place (Revelation 21). The 'bride', that is, the church, is presented in radiant splendour to take her place alongside her Husband-Redeemer, as the culmination of world history. 'She is known to him in every last detail; and he clothes her in matchless beauty. For whatever of this preparation we may see in the church as we know her today, we may thank God . . . Whatever is no part of God's permanent work should have no place among us. If it will not enhance the bride's beauty then, when she comes to share her Bridegroom's place at the marriage feast, it has no business to sully her now.' This is an important guideline for Help to remember when he encounters someone who is sullying his or her own preparation for marriage.

88

FURTHER READING

Eros Defiled by John White (IVP), ch. 5: 'The freedom that enslaves'.
Sex in the Real World by Lewis Smedes (Lion).
The Growth of Love and Sex by Jack Dominian (Darton, Longman and Todd).

The right person

Commitment of resources, lifestyle, and so on, is probably the easiest part. Commitment of the sensitive inner self into the hands of another person, without an escape clause, is the real difficulty. Hence the additional urgency to be sure that this is 'the right person'.

Much has been said on this subject by many people, without making the problem any easier. In fact, there is probably no such thing as 'the right person'. The truth lies nearer to the idea that here are two people whose love is deepening in reality (as distinct from projection), who have enough in common emotionally, intellectually, culturally, physically and spiritually to make this covenant work, and who are prepared to struggle with all the difficulties without sulking, withdrawing or fighting unfairly (using techniques of blackmail and manipulation, *etc.*).

Above all, these two people have included the Lord God in their relationship, with his Word as their guide, and his wisdom, his love and his strength in their daily life together. They then make the promise with all the attendant risks:'for better for worse . . .' When the joys are intense they will enjoy them fully, and when the hard times come (as they do in *every* relationship) they will be met with courage and hope, bearing in mind that the Lord has committed himself to his people and will help them in all their times of need.

The pronouncement that someone is 'the right person' is more convincing in retrospect, when we may also be able to detect more clearly the providential protection and guidance of God. God has given us discernment and intelligence, and, in submission to his will, he expects us to use it. Wise friends may be able to help us to see some of the wood when we are engulfed in the trees. We also need to be very sure, if we have the impression of 'rightness', that it does not just come from the relief of emotional tension brought about by 'being in love'. That can be very misleading.

It is a bit unnerving if someone says that the Lord has told him that you are the right person for him (or her). That could be emotional blackmail, and no-one should submit to it unless the Lord has spoken to *both* parties.

Masturbation

What is one to do with a normal healthy sex drive when there is no human being with whom it can be satisfied? This is a perfectly legitimate question and it gives trouble to a great many people. There are times when masturbation seems to be the only way of relieving urgent physical tension. How is Help to react to anyone who has the courage to share this problem? Actually, people do not often speak about it, but it is a difficulty for a very great number of people. Males have more trouble with this than females, usually, because of their more intense and easily aroused sexual needs; though it is common in both sexes.

The old wives' tale about insanity and other terrors have been discarded long since. For many people the need to masturbate passes when the opportunity for sexual release in marriage presents itself. The danger inherent in masturbation is its tendency to be habit-forming. By its very nature it is a solitary activity, usually accompanied by fantasies which one can stimulate by oneself. This can become such an absorbing activity that it is easier eventually to have a private sex life, which one can control without reference to someone else, than to share with another living person who feels, loves and responds. Fantasies and artificial stimulators are no adequate substitute for people; they cannot share the joys, fears and intimacies.

A withdrawn person who experiences human relationships as difficult can find an all-too-easy 'solution' in masturbation. Perhaps such a person is at greatest risk of becoming a prey to the habit. The danger is that he will learn to retreat into his own private world rather than venture out into real heterosexual relationships. A great deal of emotional energy can be used in masturbation and fantasies. It is wise not to allow it a central place in the thought-life.

One of the crushing burdens associated with this is the sense of guilt, as we have said already. This sense can be relieved by the realization that masturbation need be only a passing phase. The pressure is then removed and the subject can be prayed over and controlled with greater realism. Chronic and obsessional masturbation could be a symptom of deep insecurity or sexual inhibitions.

Help will bear these things in mind as he and his friend try to wrestle with this problem. His friend may be doing a good cover-up job and hiding his inner vulnerability. Help will try to enable him to emerge from his inner withdrawn world and to relate more openly to other people, in order that appropriate sexual release may eventually become a possibility. Christian people will be striving towards whole-ness which includes control of one's own body and natural urges, sexually and in every way. They will also remember that the sexual urge is God-given and, at some times in life, enormously powerful. Help must aim, with his friend, to be holding these things in balance.

FURTHER READING
My Beautiful Feeling by Walter Trobish (Editions Trobish).
Eros Defiled by John White (IVP), ch. 4: 'Sex on a desert island'.

Homosexuality
One of the symptoms of our age is the overt interest in homosexuality. Homosexuality has been around for thousands of years. Why is it only now receiving such attention in our culture? Help needs to think about some of the basic principles so that he does not become confused by uninformed talk on the subject.

We are left in little doubt about God's purpose in the

creation of two sexes. The explicit teaching of God's Word condemns homosexual practice (Romans 1:26-27) because it is a denial of his creative intentions (Genesis 1:27-28). Therefore Help cannot condone such activity. But Help must distinguish between homosexual *orientation* and overt *practice*.

Homosexual *orientation* is generally accepted as a passing phase of adolescent development. Many people who remain stuck at the homosexual phase regret it deeply and would give much to be able to move on to heterosexual relationships. They see themselves as being not gay, but sad. They have struggled, prayed, sought help and wept, but are genuinely unable to change their basic orientation. It may or may not be attributable to genetic constitution. There is no firm evidence. It is more probably connected with the emotional environment of early childhood and defective parental relationships. Either way, a young adult may find himself facing in a direction opposite to that of the majority of people.

This will mean loneliness, which is one of the main scourges of the homosexual condition. Thus, Help's main task in this situation is to befriend, even if he cannot understand or even sympathize. It is not his job to be critical or judgmental. Help will stand by such people in love, as he would stand by anyone who has to live with some particular form of suffering.

God does not always remove a 'thorn in the flesh' (which is sometimes obvious and sometimes hidden). Sometimes we have to live with it and endure its limitations. But that is not the end of the story. In living with a 'thorn' we can learn deeply about a quality of living which is beyond ordinary experience, as paraplegic Joni Eareckson has done from her wheelchair.

That sounds so easy to say, but is so costly to do. Surely that is the meaning of 2 Corinthians 12:8-9, where Paul speaks of his own 'thorn': 'Three times I pleaded with the Lord to take it away from me. But he said to me, "My grace is sufficient for you, for my power is made perfect in weakness".' The trouble is that we prefer our own power, and are often reluctant to believe and accept that God's power is of a different type – and more effective!

There are other young people, however, who feel unsure of themselves and their sexuality. They may also have had one or two unfortunate sexual encounters, as a result of which they have decided that it is easier to relate to their own sex than to try to cope with the incomprehensible opposite sex. The social climate makes this easy nowadays, and many a person who could, with help, struggle on towards heterosexual relationships is encouraged to opt for immaturity.

Help may need to take stock of his own reactions. He may recoil in distaste from the idea of homosexuality. It is this sort of recoiling which spells such loneliness for people with a homosexual orientation. Sometimes this recoiling is connected with an almost unrecognized fear of contamination. That, surely, reflects a certain lack of secure confidence in Help's own sexuality. He will need to think and pray about this, seeing his friend as a person with human needs. In this way Help will be able to reach out and offer what love and support is appropriate.

The whole subject of homosexuality is complex. It includes the matter of loving relationships as well as sexual activity. Help should acquaint himself with some of the written material on this subject if he wants to understand it more fully.

FURTHER READING
The Homosexual Way: A Christian Option? by David Field (IVP).
Christian Attitudes to Homosexuality by Peter Coleman (SPCK).

CONCLUSION

When Help is thinking generally about his task, he will need to avoid the optimistic view of human nature adopted by much humanistic psychology promulgated by Maslow, Fromm and others. He will avoid the pessimistic view of the nihilistic existential thinkers like Camus and Sartre. He will also avoid the behaviourist approach of Skinner and others who maintain that we are products of stimulus-response and have no power of choice and little ability to control our environment.

Help will hold to the biblical concept of man which sees the ambiguity of our nature in terms of the doctrines of creation, the fall, and redemption. He will, therefore, view himself and his friends with the optimism of God's redemptive grace of forgiveness, hope and restoration to the position of sons: God making himself available at our point of need. God sometimes makes himself available directly, and sometimes through other people. Our God knows what suffering is about. He has been there too. He has entered into human pain for the purposes of redemption. Therefore he is not untouched by the feeling of our infirmities and he knows how to comfort and strengthen.

When the writer to the Hebrews exhorted his fellow Christians to 'spur one another on to . . . good deeds' (Hebrews 10:24) he was surely meaning more than an increased amount of worthy activity. I cannot help feeling that the word 'deeds' means activity of the spirit as well as of the body. If anyone aspires to be a Help the first essential prerequisite is time spent alone with God, in silence, giving him a chance to speak (not bombarding him with our thoughts and petitions), allowing him to search our own hidden life and receiving his goodness, his truth and his healing.

The word 'help' means to exhort, to come alongside, to comfort, to make strong, to encourage or to enable. Most of us can do this if we put our minds to it. Shall we let Paul have the last word? 'We have different gifts . . . If a man's gift is . . . serving, let him serve . . . if it is encouraging, let him encourage . . . if it is contributing to the needs of others, let him give generously . . . if it is showing mercy, let him do it cheerfully' (Romans 12:6-8).

May God help us to help others!

Surely God is my help; the Lord is the one who sustains me (Psalm 54:4)

You, O Lord, have helped me and comforted me (Psalm 86:17)

Unless the Lord had given me help, I would soon have dwelt in the silence of death (Psalm 94:17)

Do not fear, for I am with you; do not be dismayed, for I am your God. I will strengthen you and help you; I will uphold you with my righteous right hand (Isaiah 41:10)

Blessed is he whose help is the God of Jacob, whose hope is in the Lord his God (Psalm 146:5)

Because he (Jesus) himself suffered when he was tempted, he is able to help those who are being tempted (Hebrews 2:18)